ANAND RAJ RANA'S

WINDING WHISKER
FEW MOLES OF DIM LIFE

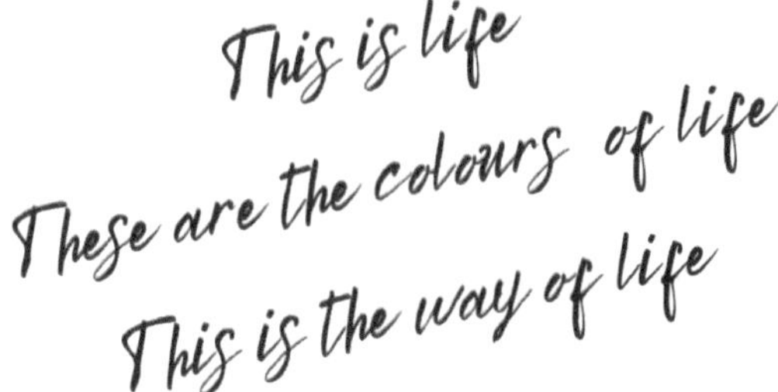

-To every human alive

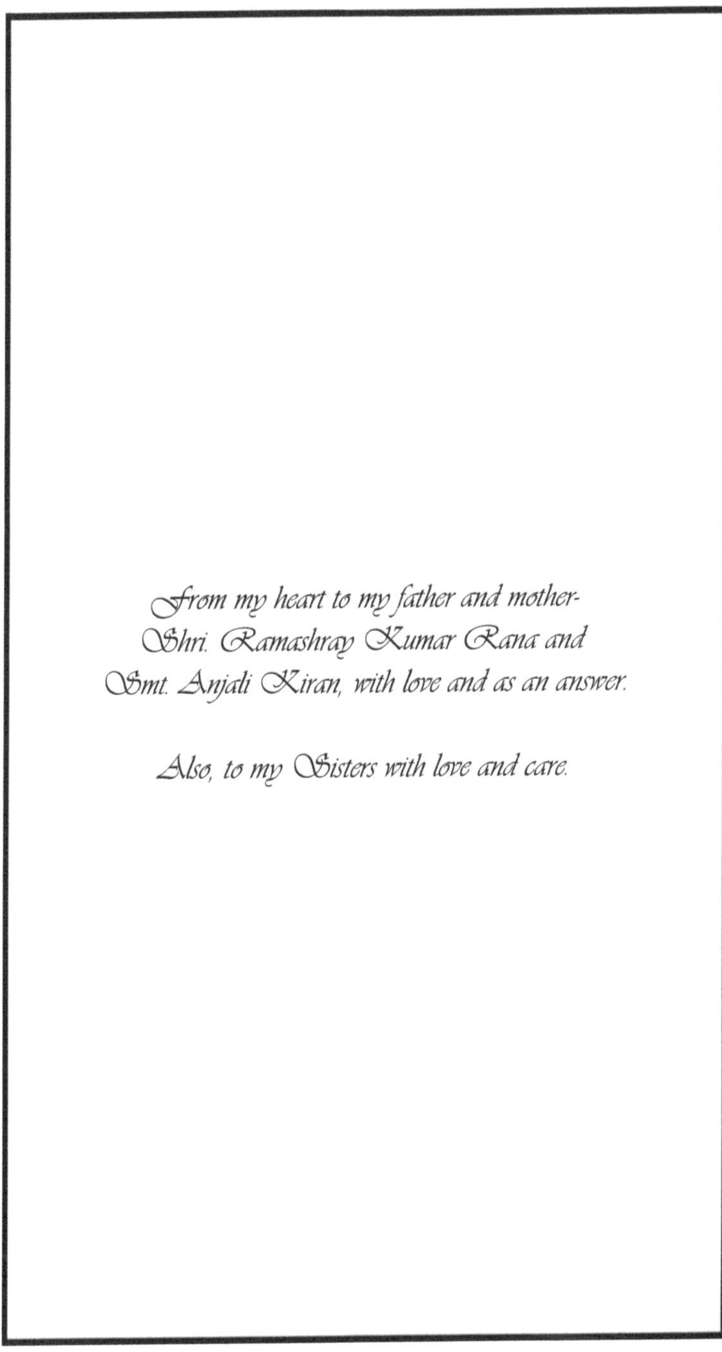

From my heart to my father and mother-
Shri. Ramashray Kumar Rana and
Smt. Anjali Kiran, with love and as an answer.

Also, to my Sisters with love and care.

Contents

SUTRA 1

What is Death?

A question of all,
But no answer to solve.
To live, we die every day.
Is it death?
Or when we die, a day to live again, is it death?

Is stained with blood, buried in mud,
Burning in hurt, or living in death called death?
Or dying to live a peaceful life called death?
What is death?
If one kills a bad guy by mistake,
The person who was bad, but the killer is a taboo.
But when on the battlefield one kills millions who were good,
They get a medal for killing someone.
Fighting to kill,
Or die trying? Called death.

What is death but a gentle breeze,
A whisper through the autumn trees,
A fleeting shadow in the night,
A star that fades from mortal sight.

It's the soldier on the battlefield,
A final breath, a shield unsealed.

The nurse who holds a cooling hand,
As souls slip to another land.

Is it the hush at twilight's end,
A final note that chords extend,
A bridge we cross to realms unseen,
Where dreams and waking interweave.
Is it a choice of good or bad art,
To the dead end or to a new start.

What is death but a tranquil sleep,
A promise we are meant to keep,
A journey past the known terrain,
Where loss gives way to peace, not pain.

It's the mother's tears, the father's grief,
The orphaned child in disbelief.
It's the poet's pen that writes no more,
The artist's brush that paints the shore.

It's the end of a start,
Or the start of the world's greatest art.
What is it?

Is it the echo of a song,
That lingers though the singer's gone,
A chapter closed in life's great tome,
A call to rest, to find our home.

What is death but life transformed,
A cycle in which we are born,
Not an end, but a new start,
A journey to make of a new art.

What is Death?

10

DELViNG DEEP

It's a simple truth that everything has an end. The ultimate end for every living being is symbolised by the word "Death". But have you ever wondered if a question has ever arisen in any one of the 86 billion cells of your complex mind: "What is Death?" This poem wrestles with the unsung concept of death, exploring its myriad interpretations and implications. It poses profound questions about the nature of death and contrasts various perspectives on what it might mean.

The poem opens with a philosophical inquiry into the essence of death, questioning whether it represents an end or a new beginning. It reflects on the seemingly contradictory nature of death-whether it signifies a mark of violence and loss or a step toward a peaceful existence. The central question is: "What is it?"

Through vivid imagery and poignant examples, the poem contrasts the perception of death in different contexts. It delves into the complexity of death, touching on themes of violence, morality, and the divergent ways in which society responds to acts of killing. This work questions the inconsistency between how death is perceived in wartime versus in personal or criminal contexts.

The poem then shifts to a more contemplative tone, presenting death as a gentle and natural transition. It links death to a breeze, a shadow, or a fading star, portraying it as an inevitable and serene part of existence. It also tries to evoke the imagery of a final breath, a cooling hand, and a peaceful sleep, suggesting that death might be a journey toward peace rather than pain.

In the end, it conveys the profound truth that death is not an end but a transformation-a cycle that leads to a new beginning. It portrays death as a continuation of life's journey, an opportunity to embrace a new phase rather than a final conclusion. At last, an important but unsolved question remains, and the question is asked from every living creature: "What is Death?"

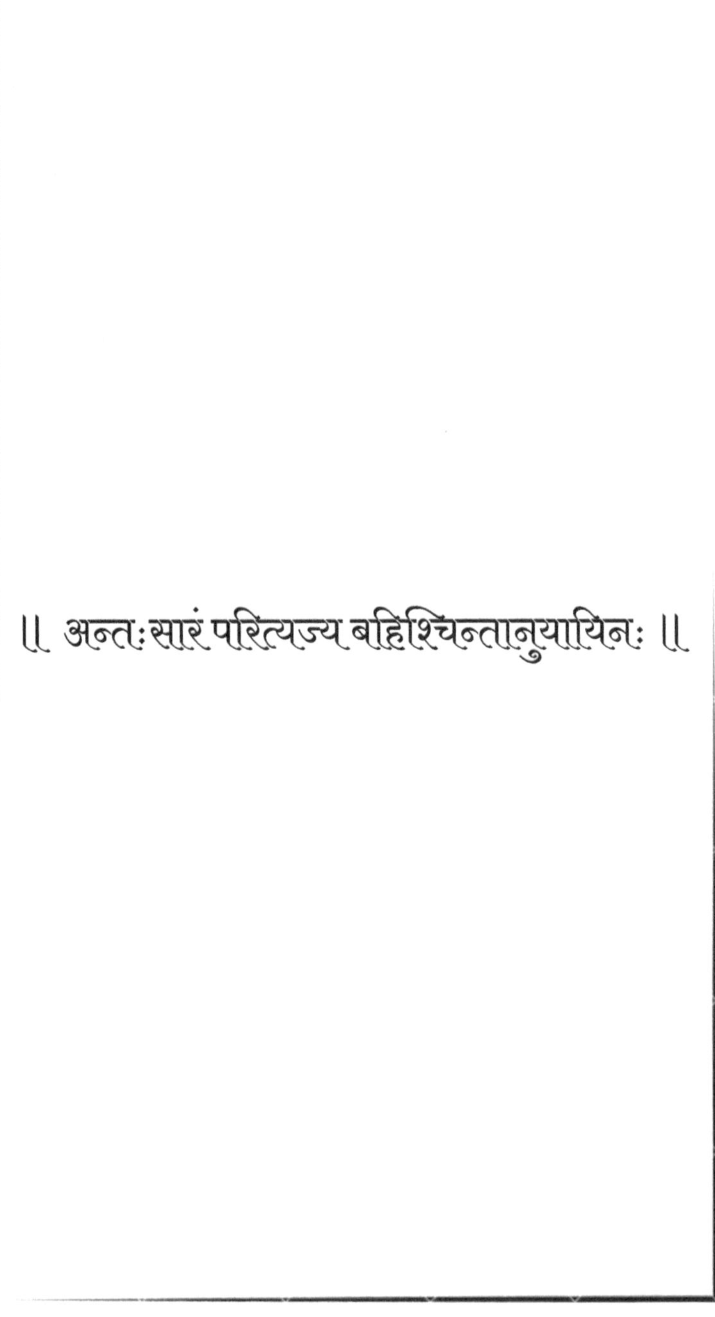

॥ अन्तःसारं परित्यज्य बहिश्चिन्तानुयायिनः ॥

SUTRA 2

Rich Life v/s "Rich" Life

It's glowing white,
In the ambers of sunkissed light.
Birds humming in their homes of calm.
Chirp, Tweet, Warble, Trill, Caw...
Caw, Tweet, Trill, Chirp...
With every chirp, a light takes flight,
The meadow dances in weaving bright.

A Lambo pale, stops at sign, with blaze on Street,
A roaring sun with wheels as feet.
A gold rush, a tune of bliss,
Nothing's need, a beauty life's kiss.

A man of lies, driving the life,
On the horizon, flowing on dim.
"The life's so beautiful in this shitty ash."
Going on, in his mind in flash.

With a flash of white, he nods to right,

To find the lies, buried alive.
'A man of life, holding...a tiny hand tight,
Other hand of cute, hold by a mist of fog.
Three souls of life, playing in park's light.
A doll's sweet smile on the swing tight,
The body of lost, pushing the laugh.
The angel with strength, fills the joy,
In the arms of calm, they all reside.'
Birds swimming high,
All life forms, of heaven to lord,
Enjoying, delighting in the meadow wind.
Till their clocks tick their last.
Chirp, Tweet, Warble, Trill, Chirp...

The soul turns around from the swing,
His face of man, laughing so loud.

Suddenly, the horn...blows around.
The man closes eyes on the gold,
Takes a breath, smells till his soul.
A smile of calm, flows on face,
A rest of all, residing in heart's breast.

The wheels of dreams turn around to reside,
Leaving a life in the nest of unsung paradise.

जीवनं कदापि सिद्धं न भवितुम् अर्हति।

DELVING DEEP

....

Life is a paradox wrapped in illusions. We often chase the golden mirage, believing wealth, status, and luxury to be the ultimate keys to happiness. But amidst the blinding blaze of material riches, a different kind of wealth exists-one that cannot be bought, only felt. A wealth many of us forget during the journey.

This poem is a journey through contrast, weaving the radiant yet deceptive glow of a luxurious life with the quiet, unspoken beauty of a truly rich existence. An existence lost in the golden pages of our beautiful life.

The poem begins with nature-pristine and untouched. The golden sun blesses the earth, birds hum their eternal symphony, and the meadow sways in harmony with life. This is wealth in its purest form-peace, simplicity, and the untainted joy of existence.

Then enters the world of artificial brilliance: a pale Lamborghini, roaring down streets paved with desires. A man, surrounded by everything, yet distant from meaning, races toward a false paradise. The gleam of gold blinds him, making him believe he has captured beauty itself. But has he? Or is he merely driving through the ashes of something lost?

A moment of revelation unfolds-a fleeting vision of truth. A man, untouched by luxury, holds the hands of love and innocence. A child's laughter, the warmth of a guiding embrace, the echoes of life playing beneath the soft glow of a park's light-these are the riches that cannot be measured...can't be bought...only lived. This is where the soul breathes freely.

The man in the Lamborghini, lost in his illusion, takes a breath, inhaling deeply-not the scent of burning ambition, but something purer. And in that moment, he smiles. Not for the gold, not for the roaring engine beneath him, but for the glimpse of a paradise he unknowingly left behind.

As the wheels turn once more, he doesn't chase the mirage any more. Instead, he leaves behind the world of false grandeur, returning-perhaps too late-to the forgotten nest of unsung paradise.

For true riches are not in the shine of metal, but in the glow of moments lost between heartbeats.

जीवनं कदापि सिद्धं न भवितुम् अर्हति।

|| चरन्मार्गोन्विजानाति ||

SUTRA 3

So lucky was She

So good life was it,
When we lived together.
But that bloody second,
Destroyed every end.
This is a story of love and loss,
Of a brother and sister who paid the cost.

The world was full of dead.
When in a home bide two hearts beat.
Back in the days, life was swell,
Together we dwelled in our wooded shell.
Life was real gold, you know,
Me and my sweet sis in a small house, just so.
They loved each other with all their hearts.
They vowed to never be apart.
A sibling pair, like chicks in chest,
Not in coop, but in a cosy nest,
Monsters and ghosts, their secret guests.

In the heart of green they bide, we called it home,
Creatures lurked around, we weren't alone.
Love filled our home, a shield so strong,

Yet shadows danced, where we belong.

It was a special day, her birthday bright,
I warned her of shadows, of ominous light.
But free-spirited, she took a chance,
Into the shadows, stepped where phantoms dance.
I was out getting wood for some yummy food,
Door open, she thought all was good.
Into the clutches of spirits so sly,
A brother late, so desperate cry.
World is full of dead, I warned her, but she didn't see,
Out she came, thought I was near, silly as can be.

Saw her coming out, such a chilling sight,
In the grasp of ghosts, a helpless fight.
Ran to save her, woods dropped from my hand,
But I stumbled, fell on the haunted land.
Ghostly hands grabbed, flew her into the shadows dark,
I ran to catch her, a futile embark.
Long sharp nails, they put in me,
Left with her shoe, a memory to be.
Please help me, God.
Creator of us, the Earth's lord.
He cried out for the reply,
Which he never got, a tragic fact relay.

He then embarked on a quest, through woods so wild,
To find his love, lost in dark tides,
Fighting monsters and ghosts, like a wounded child.
A journey full of flesh and blood, oh my,
Fighting, struggling high, but he didn't wanna say goodbye.
A river under Crocs he crossed.
His body with one leg, the other cut off.

Under a tree, I rested, for blood ahead.
Hugged her shoe, cried so hard,
Tree turned monster, attacked me in the yard.
Tried to consume me in the bright dark,
With axe in hand, I fought the gloom.
Cut off its stream, escaped from the loop,
Kept on going, my journey reshaped.
Escaped with scars, he continued the ride,
One leg less, but love as his guide.

After all the struggle, he finally got to her,
Face all scared, a painful eye blur.
One leg less, fingers left four,
One arm broken down, body all torn.
Destination reached, with body full of pain,
Tried so hard, but all in vain.

Tried hard to save her, my heart did shout,
Ate and threw her, a monstrous brute.
Watched her being eaten, thrown, broken,
Tried so hard, words left unspoken.
Her body full of blood, her body torn apart,
Anger on face, his eyes turned dark.
He halted the monsters with rage,
With fire in eyes, to put them in cage.
But they beat him, put in him their nails,
Pushed him in dark, they ran in embark.
With great difficulty, he crawled to her,
Leaving blood road behind, a constant flowing guilt.
Eyes full of pain a reservoir with tears filled.
I couldn't save her, felt the loss,
Life ended, on my chest she tossed.

One who was a bad dream for ghosts,
Couldn't save his life from lost.
In the end, she met a fate so Grim,
Love lost, shadows won, in a forest Dim.

DELViNG DEEP

This poem weaves a tale of a world in my heart, which tells the story of a life made in imagination born from the stark realities of today's world. Deeply rooted by realities of the current universe we live in. It took 100,000 minutes of my life to create this piece of art, and such dedication speaks volumes about its significance. Every word in this poem is a reflection of truth and reality, imbued with profound meaning. It stands as one of my most cherished creations, a mirror of our world crafted from the depths of my heart.

The dark, deadly, bloody forest symbolises today's world, encapsulating the essence of human civilization. The poem begins in this deep forest, a realm of lost hope and boundless darkness, a shadow that engulfs all. This forest represents the legacy of our species- The Homo sapiens, envisioned through a lens of darkness of heart.

Nestled near this ominous forest is a small house, representing ordinary, vulnerable humans-like a flickering candle in a pitch-black room. This house shelters two lights ready to shine upon the world: a brother and a sister. The brother, may inferred to be a police officer or soldier as evil forces do nothing to him and are afraid of him, embodies protection and strength. The poem unfolds in this deep, dark forest, a reflection of a society where darkness prevails and light is scarce.

The forest teems with creatures-some benevolent, others malevolent. Yet, it is the ghosts and monsters that dominate, symbolising the corrupt and malevolent individuals in our society who wreak havoc. Within this forest, the small house of the brother and sister stands as a beacon of hope and light for a brighter future. The brother, older and braver, ventures into the forest. The ghosts and monsters, representing the malevolent forces of society, fear him because he symbolises justice and authority. As he can cage these evil forces and is like a bad dream for them.

One fateful day, the flower-like sister, believing her brother is near and all is safe, steps out of the house. Tragically, she is captured by the ghosts, symbolic of society's oppressive forces. Despite the brother's desperate attempts to save her, his efforts prove futile and met the face of grim. He embarks on a perilous journey through the forest, battling various monsters and ghosts that represent societal issues like corruption and political malfeasance. The tree in the poem symbolises forces like politicians who seek to obstruct his path.

In the journey, he loses a leg, representing the backlash offered in today's world, but the brother's resolve remains unshaken as he continues his quest and, at last, crosses the dark dead. However, upon reaching his sister, he finds her brutally torn apart by the monsters. His heroic efforts culminate in tragedy, with his sister dying in his arms. The brother fights against the monsters, who eventually flee, leaving a trail of blood, represents the relentless struggle against society's evils.

This poem is a profound reflection of today's world, capturing the timeless battle between good and evil. It is a reflection of increasing rape cases on our earth and their results. It conveys the courage and determination required to confront darkness, even when the odds seem insurmountable. This is the essence of the poem and the reason behind my dedication to crafting it-to unveil these deeper meanings and truths about our heavenly planet turning into hell.

28

।। एतानि सर्वाणि कालः समीक्षते ।।

SUTRA 4

This is the Story off!

Bzzzz...bzzzz...
Hello!
'Hello...hello...Are you Alive?'
Yep, buddy, beautiful in my life.
'I think there's something wrong,'
No buddy, everything's a flop,
Beautiful, chill, stress-free, ha...ha.
'No, you are in trouble, tell me bro, I will help as much as I can, so,'
All's perfect, dude...no problems in life,
It's beautifully dark, bright.

'No, you're in mental trouble, share it...I know.'
No...I am not...
No...No...No...
And with an instance, the Black turned White,
Everything vanished from my unsung sight.
Flowing through the veins, we all at once,
From top to toe to heart to brain.
Excuse me, blood, your last stop has arrived,

Do you know what it is in your sight?
The heart, sitting alone in the back of the bus,
In the tough body, a beautiful hush.
Tick...tock...tick...tock...tick...
'What do you want?
What do you want, tell me...tell me...'
Nothing! No! Nothing! Aaaaa...
Tick...tock...tick...tock...tick...

Wait a second,
Where are We?
This is the story of what,
Is it bullshit or a piece of Art?
Is this real or a deleted part?
This is the story of What?

Tick...tock...tick...tock...tick...
Bzzzz...bzzzz...
Hello!
Nothing!
Aaaaa...
Tick...tock...tick...tock...tick...
Your Stop has arrived,
A Voice speaks high.
The Red Heart laughing at the back, sitting by.
Back of the bus, like a King,
But there's no one to see him.
This is such a tale of grim,
Oh my goodness, it's so brightly dim.
Tick...tock...tick...tock...tick...
'Hello...Are you okay? Don't worry, I am always with you.'
I want no one in my life, sue.
Leave me alone in this beautiful hue.

'Bro, you're in mental trouble,
Don't worry, I am always with you, and will be, no matter
what.'
I am okay...OK.

"Dude, Are you Alive?"
In an instant, the world starts to break,
From veins to cells to the big bang stars,
Mind walks the whole bars,
In an instance of pursuit,
No, it's a shit parasite.

With everything roaming around,
We come to the point, making the round.
It's dark before my eyes,
Sitting on the bed with disguise.
Everything around, a person needs from top to bottom in a
cosy sheet.

What just happened?
What was it?
Tick...tock...tick...tock...tick...
I directed my cornea to the beautiful wall,
What's the time of my soul?
It's the midnight of an era glow,
It's the start of a hue show.
What just happened in front of my eyes?
Was it real or a dream in disguise?
The room smells so nice, the bed so cosy,
Everything around is what's so nasty.
What just happened?
Was it a dream?
Was it real?

Or,
Am I a deadly dream?
Is it true, or is it a show?
Am I true, or a...
                              35

Bzzzz...bzzzz...
The phone rings by,
Hello!

"This is the story of..."
जीवनं सिद्धम् अस्ति।

DELViNG DEEP

A tale unfinished, a sentence severed mid-thought-"This is the Story off!" speaks of abrupt endings and lost narratives. It captures the weight of words that almost were the silence, where voices should have been. The poem unfolds like a script abandoned before its climax, where meaning lingers but resolution never arrives. Here, absence is louder than presence, and what remains is not the story itself, but the void it leaves behind.

"This is the Story off!" is not just a psychological and philosophical poem, but it's a mirror of the 99% of us- Humans. It's a piece of art that intricately portrays the eternal conflict between the heart and the brain. It is a poetic exploration of rationality versus emotion, of logic versus feeling, and ultimately, of realisation that comes too late.

At its core, the poem tells a story that many souls experience in their lives- the internal war between what we think is right and what we truly feel is right. We often obey the mind's commands, dismissing the quiet, desperate whispers of the heart. But what happens when, for once, we decide to listen- only to realise that the moment has already passed?

The title, "This is the Story off!", itself holds an eerie sense of incompletion, much like the poem's message. The phrase "Story off" suggests:

-> A cut-off narrative, symbolising missed chances and unfinished emotions.

-> A disconnected call, reinforcing the imagery of the heart trying to reach out but being ignored.

-> A psychological dissonance, as if the story was there, waiting to be understood, but never fully grasped in time.

The abruptness of "off" conveys regret, severance, and the irreversible loss of a moment that could have changed everything.

Heart v/s Brain – The Call That Went Unanswered. The poem unfolds as a conversation between the brain and the heart, presented metaphorically as a phone call.

-> The heart keeps calling, urging, pleading to be heard. It represents emotions, instincts, desires, and perhaps even an ignored truth buried deep inside.

-> The brain keeps rejecting the call, choosing reason, practicality, and cold logic over passion and feeling, or love. It symbolises control, calculation, and the fear of uncertainty.

-> The turning point comes when the brain finally chooses to listen-but it's too late. The call is disconnected. The opportunity is lost. What was once a choice is now a regret. जीवनं सिद्धम् अस्ति।

This piece of art often reflects deep existential themes, and in this poem, the psychological battle between logic and feeling takes centre stage. It taps into:

-> The Human Condition: The struggle of deciding between head and heart is something everyone experiences. The poem mirrors how we suppress emotions in favour of reason, only to realise later that our feelings had their own wisdom too.

-> The Nature of Regret: It emphasises how procrastination in emotional matters leads to irreversible loss-whether it's in love, dreams, or self-discovery.

-> Symbolism of the Call: The heart's calls can represent many things- a missed opportunity, an ignored inner voice, or even someone who needed us, but whom we failed to respond to in time.

For Tone and Emotion, The poem likely carries:

-> A slow build-up of tension, with the heart continuously calling, but the brain stubbornly refusing to pick up.

-> A climax of realisation, where the brain finally acknowledges the heart's importance-but by then, it's too late.

-> A haunting silence at the end, symbolises the emptiness of missed chances.

The poem does not just tell a story-it makes the reader feel the weight of hesitation and the sting of regret.

"This is the Story off!" is a cautionary tale-a warning that sometimes, logic alone is not enough. It urges the reader to listen to their heart before the moment is lost forever.

It is not just a poem. It is a psychological mirror, making the reader question:

"What calls have I ignored? And what if, when I finally decide to answer, it's already too late?"

A story never ends where we think it does. Beneath the last page, beneath the silence after the final word, something lingers-something unresolved, something lost in the abyss of time. "This is the Story off!" is not just a poem; it is a fracture in reality, a glimpse into the hollow echoes left behind when a tale is cut short.

It is the story of all that was left unsaid, all that was erased, forgotten, or torn away before it could be understood. It is the moment when the ink smears, when the voice falters, when history is rewritten not by truth, but by silence. Every word that vanishes leaves behind a wound, and this poem bleeds with those wounds.

Here, the reader is not just an observer-they are a witness to the quiet tragedy of unfinished fates. Perhaps it is their own story, or perhaps it is the story of a world that never learned to listen. But the warning is clear: A story does not die when it's abandoned-it rots, it festers, it grows into something unrecognisable. And when it returns, it will demand to be heard.

This is the story that was never told. This is the story that should have been. This is the story off.

|| यत् पश्यसि तत् त्वयि अस्ति ||

SUTRA 5

Death below my Sleep

In the stillness of a room, a tale unfolds,
Of a boy with courage, his story to be told.
Beneath my bed, a creature resides,
A deadly monster with hunger that abides.

Its skin, a mosaic of shadows and scales,
Eyes like embers, where darkness prevails.
Blood on its teeth, a sinister grin,
A flesh-eating nightmare, lurking within.

From another planet, it descended unknown,
In search of prey, a world to call its own.
A cosmic intruder, in shadows it hides,
Feeding on fear as the night abides.

I am a cute little boy, very sweet, very bold,
I like to dance, joke, and paint stories to behold.
But my favourite colour, as I've said,
Is the red where scary stories are spread.
What you don't know?

No problem, now I will share a life,
Which you will remember to forget,
But you will never be able in your sight.

Can I tell you a story, not so old?
But one that's chilling, leaves you cold.

I lived in a small house with my sweet mother and father
bitter old.
My room was on the second floor.
Under my bed, there lived a soul,
Pretty sweet but old.

A month ago, in my room alone,
I warned him, yet he was drawn.
I warned him a lot but he peeped down the bed,
What could be done, he caught his head,
He was not his enemy,
Whatever, it was his destiny.
Then never I saw him, listened only his scream,
His head, his legs, his eyes apart,
His blood shattered on the floor a lot.

He feasted him to fill his tummy,
His head is ghost but very chubby,
Dark face, head cut sharp,
Eyes red like lava dark.
Mouth a pit, teeth long and sharp,
Sips red juice sweet leaves a mark.
Do you know what he says?
I asked him a day "Reveal your tale, creature of the light,
Why haunt my life, why give the world such fright?"
The monster's reply, a growl from the abyss,

"I am but a reflection, of the fears you cannot dismiss."
"I like blood, I like to die,
I like to kill, I like baby's cry."

He says his soul came from misery,
But the rich are not as sweet as he.
From another world, he whispers his need,
A creature of terror, born to feed.

From another planet, he came he said,
I don't know but other earth he says.
I am the guy who seeks him high,
But people say it's my mind's eye.

I was talking to him,
When she climbed the stairs, unaware,
The truth beneath the bed, she did dare.
No bloody rascal is under your bed,
It's only dust in your head.
I warned her but she repeated again,
You know what happened then.
Poor luck.
She screamed, she begged,
But dragged below the bed.

Police siren horns down.
Surrender, we know you're there,
Identify him if you dare.
Real or imagined, sweet or dread,
A mystery lingers in words unsaid.

The voice echoed once again,
"We know who he is," they say with might,

But truth or fiction, hidden in the room,
Am I the hero, or the villain in your sight?
Sweet, calm, polite or a deadly friend right?
Innocent child, or creature of fright?

DELViNG DEEP

At first glance, "Death Below My Sleep" may appear perplexing, but every word within it holds profound significance. The narrative revolves around a young, quirky, and endearing boy whose experiences unveil deeper truths about the human psyche.

The demon, or monster, depicted in the poem serves as a metaphor for the inner demons that reside within each of our brains. It symbolises the inner struggles, fears, and complexities of the human mind as the boy grapples with his own personal demons.

As the demon claims to hail from another planet, it metaphorically represents the depths of our own brains. This marks that our minds are vast, complex worlds teeming with both good and evil forces. Just as the boy's mother said, "No bloody rascal is under your bed, It's only dust in your head," it's a question for us all to identify the reality of the type of demons we face within ourselves: good or evil? Ask yourself.

The boy's dilemma raises profound questions about the nature of good and evil within us. Despite his unsung efforts to warn his parents about the monster under his bed, they fail to heed his warnings. This highlights the challenges of communication and understanding between individuals, even within familial relationships.

If you stop and think, the boy questions us at the end: Who is he? What did he do? Was it good? Was it bad? Is he a hero or a villain? Was his approach right? Did he do something wrong? If you believe he did wrong, then how? He politely asked his parents not to yell, but they didn't listen. He never hurt them. Plus, he was just a kid. If he had tried to save his parents, maybe the monster would have hurt him too. He did his best to warn them. It's a question for everyone. Think about it: What kind of thoughts linger in your mind? Was the boy's action okay or not? Was he doing the right thing? Was the monster real or just a scary thought? Is the boy real or just part of imagination?

|| शुद्धं प्रेम सर्वदा हृदि वसति ||

SUTRA 6

Drawing her Ghost

See...
Her eyes of Amber,
Her face so bright.
Shining my soul,
As a smooth light.
So Bright.

Do you know, the days of warm,
Two mocking souls in a cute nest whole.

The sky is pale,
The sun is light.
Embracing sight at unsung height.

Chirp...Coo...Coo...Chirp....
In the garden of green fresh souls,
With a canvas blank, I sit.
Drawing her beauty,

In an instance of sight, I see.
Rays of sour, beautifying the soul,
Beams of white, gathering the green.
On a table, I sit,
Burying her white on the canvas white,
Not white, but colourful in my unsung sight.
Chirp...Coo...Coo...Quack...Chirp....

You see, what I saw.
The voice of sky, swimming in the red,
Breath in stock, sleeping on cosy bed.
The canvas burning hard, on my face.
I sit with my pen, smiling so hard.
See...red fire brightening my face,
Flowing out of the white,
Now filled with colours of light.

She, standing in front of me,
Smiling so sweet.
Her face of amber,
Angel from heaven, queen of hearts.
Eyes of gold, red sweet cheeks,
The mole on her neck, glasses on her nose.
The fuel of me, white blood Roar...Roar.

Caw...Caw...Screech...Hoot...
I drew her so beautiful,
You wanna see the picture I drew,
Burning white in my hand,
The art of dead, only I drew.

DELViNG DEEP

See...the art of dead, drawn by the hands of the living heart. A picture painted, not with mere colours, but with the soul itself. A silent tale of white, burning in the grasp of time.

A canvas sits bare, an empty echo of longing, waiting to be filled-not with mere strokes of colour, but with the essence of a soul. The poet sees her-not just in memory, but in the air itself, in the warmth of days past, in the lingering touch of light on skin. Her amber eyes, her gentle glow, not merely remembered but resurrected in the silent embrace of art.

She was there once. Not in just memory, but in air, in light, in warmth. The mocking sky of red, the chirps of unseen lives, all whispering her name. The golden eyes, the amber face, the soft, sweet laugh-etched in sight, breathing in space.

Yet, The Art is Cruel. It teases the artist with a glimpse of what once was, only to remind him of what can never be again. The strokes of his pen, once alive with vibrance, now burn like embers in the cold. The colours, so carefully painted, twist into the red of a distant fire-glowing, consuming, erasing.

A table, a canvas, a man with a pen. The world fading into a single thought. With each stroke, a heartbeat. With each shade, a breath. A vision not just seen, but felt. A dream bleeding into reality, or perhaps, reality dissolving into a dream.

And there she stands...perfect. Alive in the whispers of ink, in the warmth of colour. The eyes of gold, the mole on her neck, the glasses resting on her nose-so close, so real. The masterpiece of a soul longing for its lost light.

Real, yet not. A vision born from longing, from a desperate attempt to hold onto the fleeting warmth of her smile. Every detail-her golden gaze, the mole on her neck, the glasses resting on her nose-etched in the mind of the artist, yet never to be touched. The ghost of his creation lingers for a breath, then fades, leaving only the ashes of a masterpiece that could never truly bring her back.

Then, the fire.

Not of destruction, but of truth. The white burns, the red glows, the picture folds into the embers of time. A work so perfect, too perfect to exist. The hands hold the remains, the eyes watch the ashes fly.

Because ghosts are not meant to be drawn. They are meant to be felt, to be seen in the echoes of silence, in the warmth of a forgotten sun, in the weight of a name never spoken aloud.

And so, the art fades. But the artist...He Still Sees.

|| धर्मेण हीनाः पशवः समानाः ||

SUTRA 7

DasisHam

Hello, how are you, brother dear?
I sent you something, free and clear.
An MMS of Swati, our neighbour fair,
Tell me, how is she? Just look and share.
Don't ask where it came to be,
I sent it to the group, just see.

In a world so bright, there's dark we find,
A man on blood-red stairs, confined.
I stand close by, witness it all,
"How is she?" a voice does call.
Emerging from my vocal cords,
"Yes, see her," he replies in words.

Ravan!

"What Ravan?" he asks, surprised.
The first head of Ravan: lust's despise.
Ravan violated women in flesh and bone,
Now we do it through the phone.

"What the hell, why tell me this? Tell the sender,
what's my miss?"
Words reach my ears anew,
"Would you send it if she were your sister too?"
"Aa, you!" he shouts in anger hot,
Ravan's second head: anger's plot.
Ravan, who would others' sisters violate,
Got enraged when his sister met her fate.

Third head: Moha, delusion's snare,
Fourth: Lobha, greed's affair.
Fifth: Mada, arrogance's pride,
Sixth: Maatsarya, envy inside.
Seventh: Buddhi, intellect's veil,
Eighth: Manas, mind's tale.
Ninth: Chitta, consciousness' seat,
And last but not least,
Ahamkara, ego complete.

In Treta Yuga, Ravan had ten heads,
But now in one, those vices spread.

"Who are you?" he asks, afraid.
I laugh beside him, my rage displayed.

अन्तः विश्वं पश्यन्तु
सर्वं जगत् त्वत्तो उत्पद्यते।
यद् भासते यत् न प्रकाशते तत् दूरं यत् समीपस्थम्।
तद्वहिर्तत्त्वं तत्सर्वस्याभ्यन्तरम्।

"What the hell is this? Who are you?"

I reply with a smile in dim light's hue,
"We are all Ravan, through and through."

58

DELViNG DEEP

....

"We are all Ravan," is this line correct?

This poem is not just a poem but the truth of our world. This work of words is a powerful allegory exploring the nature of inner vices and moral corruption through the metaphor of the mythical demon Ravan. It uses vivid imagery and cultural references to critique contemporary ethical lapses and highlight the inherent flaws in human nature.

It's harsh and dark, but this is the truth that the world is like this. Did you understand? If not, let me explain with an example: "It should never happen to anyone, but this is the harsh reality. Imagine a rape case and a murder occurred. A man went in the candle march for the justice of what happened and for the calmness of the girl's soul. After the march ends, while returning, if a girl passes the man, then the man will turn around to see the girl, and that's the reality. I am not saying that this is the truth for all, but it reflects the dark reality for 90% of the generation, and they ask 'Why?', also Evilness doesn't even care about age. We agree or not, but this is the truth, and 'What is truth is truth and what is truth will remain truth.'"

The poem begins with a dirty request to view an inappropriate message, quickly unravelling into a deeper commentary on human behaviour. The transition from a dark meme about a neighbour to a reflection on Ravan's symbolic heads serves as a stark contrast between love and lust.

Ravan, a central figure in the Hindu epic Ramayana, is depicted with ten heads, each symbolising a different vice. The poem draws parallels between these heads and contemporary moral failures, reflecting on how these vices manifest in modern society. Lust, anger, delusion, greed, arrogance, envy, ignorance, and ego are explored through the actions and reactions of the characters, demonstrating how these flaws are not confined to mythological figures but are prevalent in our today's everyday life.

The unsung figure's response to the character's indignation-asserting that "We are all Ravan, through and through"-emphasises the universality of thought-provoking vices. This statement is a profound commentary on the human condition, suggesting that everyone harbours these negative traits to some degree. The closing lines, in Sanskrit, reflect on the nature of reality and the self, reinforcing the idea that these vices are an intrinsic part of human nature and that understanding them is crucial to self-awareness and moral improvement for itself and for society.

In essence, this poem critiques the superficiality of modern moral concerns and encourages a deeper reflection on the internal struggles that define human behaviour. By invoking the figure of Ravan and his symbolic heads, the poem effectively conveys the complexity of human vices and the necessity of confronting them within ourselves.

"If we don't change, then nothing will change, and if nothing changes, then nothing will be changed."

|| सकृद्द्विजिहीर्षोर्निरुत्तिर्भवति. न पुनश्चक्रं न
पञ्चाङ्गानि च ||

SUTRA 8

When the Sun Goes Trembling

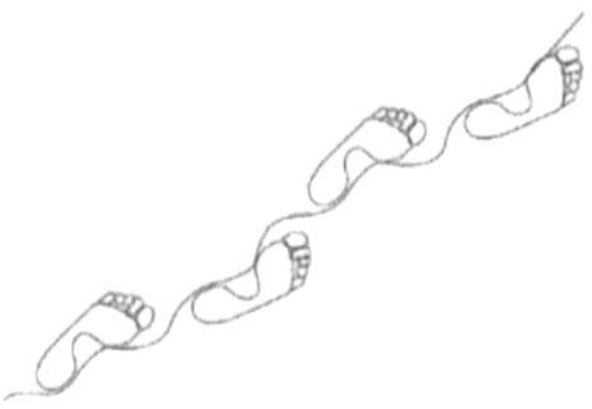

9...
When the sun goes trembling,
Run, Run, Run, Run.
When the sun goes trembling,
Run, Run, Run, Run.
No one's gonna stay alive, ha...ha...ha.
8...

They are watching.
Go to hell.
6...
"We are above the target,
Waiting for the order."
Run, Run, Run, Run.
4...
"Drop the parcel to the guests.
Happy Birthday dears."
Ha..ha..ha.
When the sun goes trembling,
Ha...ha...ha.
3...

"It's so nice day, na?
Yes, such a beautiful day."
Run, Run, Run, Run.
"Mamma, see...Something is falling from the sky!"
Run, Run, Run, Run.
Ha..ha..ha.
2...

Let's go smiling,
When the sun goes trembling,
When the sun goes trembling,
Run, Run, Run, Run.
When the sun goes trembling,
Run, Run, Run, Run, Run, Run, Run....
Find a place to hide you.
YOU are gonna vanish off.
Ha..ha..ha.

(Now I am become Death, the destroyer of worlds)
Ha...ha...ha.
0...

DELViNG DEEP

The sky breaths red, because it's full of ashes.

This tale unfolds in the thin moment between life as it is and life as it will never be again. The trembling sun becomes a false dawn- a light born not from nature, but from human hands symbolising the terrifying point where creation and destruction merge into one.

The descending numbers echo humanity's obsession with control, precision, and progress, while quietly revealing how easily existence can be measured, scheduled, and erased. Above the sky, voices speak with comfort and humour, transforming catastrophe into routine. Below, the world breathes normally- conversations continue, children wonder, and ordinary joy exists unaware of its final seconds.

This distance between those who release destruction and those who receive it reflects a painful truth of history: suffering is often delivered without hatred, only obedience.

Laughter moves through the poem like a shadow, not as happiness but as the hollow sound of power detached from consequence. It suggests a world where violence has become normal, where ending lives feels lighter than protecting them.

The closing transformation into "Death" is not of one man, but of humanity itself- the moment when humans no longer merely fight wars, but possess the ability to end worlds. The poem does not accuse a single nation or moment in time; instead, it warns of what happens when intelligence grows faster than compassion.

In the trembling sun, we do not witness the end of a city- we witness the fragile future of humanity hanging in a single breath.

The sky breaths red, and if you remove your mask...You can smell...life.

|| वसुधैव कुटुम्बकम् ||

SUTRA 9

The Code Colour

"Maa, who are they?"
They're pounding at the door.
To open it all and let shadows fall,
For mother and daughter in this room so small,
The cute room so dark, on the lava floor.
It's the tale of life written with death.
A tale of loss with glee faith.
"Sleep now, goodnight,
Nothing will happen, just be quiet."
"Maa, we're gonna die, I know they've come for me.
Let me go, or you'll too die."
"No, be quiet, or I will beat you tight."
They sit on the lava floor, to wait till die.
"Come, sleep on my thigh, let me tell you a story high."
"But Maa..."
"Be quiet, just listen."
She pats her head, calming her fears,
And begins the tale to soothe her tears.

"Once upon a time, in a forest deep and wide,
Lived a soul, pure as white, a king full of pride.
A beautiful being, a gift from the skies,
The king of all, standing tall and bright,
A creation of God, a beacon of light.

The forest was a canvas, so vibrant, so free,
A masterpiece painted for all to see.
A realm of peace, a cradle of grace,
Where every colour found its place.
On a planet called Earth,
A sight of glee.

It's a beautiful tale,
A world of peace.
A wisdom truth,
A tale of heath.

The forest, a tapestry, vibrant and free,
Each hue spoke of life's grand tale.
Each colour represents the nature's host.
A part of fall, a necessity for all:
Leaf's green, earth's brown, blue water that gleams,
Flowers in hues that light up a dream-
Pink, yellow, orange, and red,
A world where all shades beautifully spread.

But beware, my child, when the story feels gold,
When you wish to be the story's bold.
The end is a beast, dark and sly.
If not, then it's not the greatest feast.

The tale twisted, turned to despair,
Into a dead shake,
Not with milk but with blood.
The night grew cold, the air filled with fear.
White stabbed at a night harsh,
The forest echoed, covered with the sun's lust.

The body of white turned to red,
Covering the forest in a dark shade.
Other colours revolted to be the king;
They didn't want red to taste the win.
Pink waged war to turn red's fire to blush,
The Red lost the war, surrendered, and agreed to the pact,
But soon fell to brown's merciless rush.
Let pink convert due to impact.
Colours rose to seize the crown,
And the forest, my dear, began to drown.
So began the battle of shades,
A massacre where beauty fades.

One by one, the colours would fall,
Turning the forest into a lifeless sprawl.
As the days turned into night,
Only seven colours remained in sight.
At last, they clashed; they fought with all their might,
On the final day, till the forest faded into an endless night.

And when the last echo of battle cried,
Only one colour remained in sight.
And that colour, my dear, was..."

"Maa, Maa, which colour left at last? Tell why you stopped."
And with a smile dark, she gave an answer harsh.

"BLACK."

73

DELViNG DEEP

"World is so colourful, but..."

This poem is not just a group of words, but it's the harsh reality of our beautiful world. It's a mirror of the human condition and the nature of conflict through the metaphor of a colourful forest. It tries to explore the themes of faith, conflict, and the eventual dominance of darkness over the world.

The poem opens with a dark scene of a mother and daughter in a small, dark room, facing an impending threat. The daughter's fear and the mother's attempt to comfort her set the stage for the unfolding environment. The mother begins to tell a story to distract and soothe her daughter, using it as a means to both calm her fears and convey a deeper message.

The story within the poem is like paints of a vibrant picture of a forest, symbolising the world and its various religions, each represented by different colours. Initially, the forest is depicted as a harmonious and beautiful place, where each colour, or religion, contributes to a grand tapestry of peace and grace. This imagery represents the ideal of a world where different beliefs coexist in harmony.

However, the tale takes a darker turn as conflict arises. The colours, symbolising different religions or different countries, begin to fight for dominance, leading to a devastating battle. The once vibrant and peaceful forest becomes a battleground where beauty fades and life diminishes. The conflict escalates, resulting in a massacre where only seven colours remain, eventually leading to an endless, bloodied night.

The story concludes with the colour black remaining after the final battle, signifying the overwhelming dominance of darkness and the loss of diversity and peace. This powerful ending serves as a stark commentary on the destructive nature of religious and ideological conflicts and the eventual overshadowing of light by darkness.

The mother tries to save her life, her daughter from flesh-eating demons stamping at the door. This represents rape, and it showcases that, "If we don't change, then nothing will change."

In essence, the poem is an allegory of colours in a forest to address the complex and often harsh reality of global conflicts driven by dark differing beliefs like rapes and murders. It underscores the tragic outcomes of such conflicts and the profound impact they have on the world. The poem is about colours, but in reality, they are Not colours.

|| स्नेहः सर्वोत्तमं रत्नम् ||

SUTRA 10

The most Cost

What's the most expensive thing in this world wide?
Who is your hero?" he asked his dad with his sight,
Sitting in the buses last seat with words they had.
Happy on their way and conversation taking hight.

"My father, your grandfather," he met the reply,
"My father would say the brain remains,
Active for 7 minutes after you die,
And our life flashes before our eyes,
We see only those we love the most,
In their format sitting beside like ghosts."

"But I know your heroes are those actors."

He smiled, ready to let his words exit anew,
When suddenly, four terrorists roared like hue,
Shots from all sides, the bus sieged high,
Torn all apart on its way to Vaishno Devi by.

In his last 7 minutes, his life flashed by,

Days of love and moments of strife,
His first day at school, his last day at home,
And with a flash, he entered the unknown.
A new world of life, a door to be known.

He opened his eyes, lying in bed,
A blanket on top, a wet cloth on head.
Two bodies beside, their spirits so dear,
The souls of his sweet mother
And handsome father near.

He closed his eyes with their last words let go,
Entering his ears, leaving a smile to follow.
The words were:
"Don't worry, currently we are here and will always be with
you, sleep well, Good Night,"

DELVING DEEP

Have you ever asked yourself, "What is the most precious thing in your life?" or "Who is your hero?" We all desire respect from others, but there is a saying: "Who can escape from the illusion of respect? Respect is also needed for those who give seven nails in sorrow."

This poem is a poignant narrative exploring themes of love, heroism, and the transience of life through a dramatic and emotional lens. It tries to capture a moment of both profound revelation and tragedy, underscoring the fragility and value of human connections.

The poem begins with a beautiful and thought-provoking question posed by a young boy to his father about the most precious thing in the world and who his hero is. The father's response is deeply philosophical, suggesting that our minds retain the image of our loved ones for seven minutes after death and that these loved ones appear beside us like comforting spirits. This response hints at the profound emotional connections that define our lives and ultimately suggests that real heroism is found in the enduring presence of those we love more than ourselves.

As the poem flows, the scene shifts abruptly to a tragic event: a terrorist attack on a bus. The boy's life is violently interrupted, and he experiences a rapid succession of memories in his final moments-a poignant journey through significant life events and emotional touchstones. This dramatic shift from the philosophical to the tragic serves to highlight the sudden and often unpredictable nature of life and death.

In the aftermath of the attack, the boy finds himself in a liminal space between life and death. He awakens to find his parents' spirits beside him, offering him comfort and reassurance. Their final words to him, "Don't worry, we are here now and will always be with you, sleep well, goodnight," serve as a tender farewell that underscores the enduring nature of love and support from those we cherish.

The poem elegantly contrasts the abstract concept of heroism with the tangible and intimate reality of family bonds. The father's initial philosophical musing about heroes is juxtaposed with the boy's immediate experience of violence and loss, ultimately reinforcing the notion that true heroism lies in the enduring presence and love of those closest to us.

In sum, the poem is a reflective meditation on the essence of life, the fragility of existence, and the eternal nature of love. It eloquently captures the transition from the ordinary to the extraordinary, highlighting the comfort and continuity that our true loved ones provide even in the face of life's most harrowing moments. It concludes with a resonant question for all: "What is the most precious thing in your life?"

|| संसारः चक्रवत् परिवर्तते ||

SUTRA 11

Life Under my Toes

What's the status of this planet in this universe wide?
How it changed from the beginning when God made it all,
To the present situation, to its fall from rise.

I touched down on Earth, soil under my toes,
Everything was beautiful, From verdant greens to azure blues,
Every moment unfolded, in reverse, I peruse.
Because it was Destroyed, I who triggered the cataclysmic
hue.
To simple life from man in play,
To stone age from ai on way.
I ended it all, following your grand command.
Then saw in rewind the whole process of mine.
From becoming living to puppets in a play live,
I saw from end to start, each turning page.
From turning into debris to making of an art.
From end of your art to beginning of its start.

I saw the decline of life, making it complex from simple.
From plants and insects to bacteria and algae,
From birds and mammals to reptiles and fish,
From humans from apes to monkeys their start.

How they converted so fast so hard.

I saw the decrease of civilization, from space to Stone Age,
From agriculture and gathering to hunting and trade.
From science and technology to writing and art,
From politics and democracy to following religion from deep of
heart.
To homo habilis drawing their start,
From homo sapiens showing their end as an art.

Earth is now so pure and clean,
Converted to a shining gem, a sight that can be seen.
From machines loud to nature's music sweet,
Changes in scenes, oh man, was wild then.
Future people's heart is a real gold, you know,
Past they were acting like demons in the show.

Creatures you created, once humble and sweet,
Were some extinct or some on road that cannot be beat.
To kindness and love from fights and hate,
Earth's got a dual vibe, it's all the human trait.

Now, it is simple, life's grand debut,
Before was complex, everywhere you look it had grown.
Tech's flying high, goals reaching the sky,
Machines in the water, pollution reaching high.
Darkness lurked around, time's ticking by.

People's hearts turned to a mysterious song,
From caring and sharing to things going wrong.
But love still shines, like stars in the night,
Cutting through the darkness, bringing back the lost light.

Animals evolved, it's nature is seen,
To ancient fossils from creatures we know.
But progress had a cost, it's took a toll,
On homes for animals, was a heavy scroll.

So, I am back to narrate a story for you,
Which's real, not an imagination for you.
To tell Earth's story, creatures, and what it means.
In your presence, I lay it all out,
Grant them wisdom, erase their doubt.

Help man in this cosmic sea,
To protect this Earth, the gem you gave them to be.
From start to carve the gem,
And make it as beautiful as heaven.

I saw end to start,
From Earth's end from Big Bang start,
From destroyed end to making of an art.
From my eyes my age minus billion but yours a second.
Now at last I have completed the quest,
Please leave me so I can live my life rest.
And begin the work of a great past.
Become the start of your unsung art.

DELViNG DEEP

It's a universal truth that everything born will eventually meet an unsung end. Similarly, whether we think about it or not, our Earth will also meet its fate. This poem is a cosmic journey, intertwining themes of time, creation, and destruction. It recounts the journey of a divine figure, a messenger of God sent to Earth. He steps on the heavenly soil of Earth, which has been turned into hell. To end it all, he finishes it, much like the Kalki avatar of Vishnu, as described in the Kalki Purana by Shri Agastya and Shri Vishvamitra between 1500 and 1700 CE. Kalki will be the tenth avatar of Vishnu and will end Kalyug by fighting Kali, restarting the cycle.

The poem opens with a question, pondering the status of Earth in the grand universe and reflecting on how the planet has evolved since its inception. The speaker, an almost divine figure, recounts their experience of rewinding Earth's history after triggering its destruction, witnessing the world move backwards from its chaotic modern state to a simpler, purer beginning.

The poem masterfully explores contrasts: the rise and fall of civilization, the complexity of life returning to simplicity, and the transformation from a technologically advanced world to a more peaceful, nature-driven existence. It touches on human progress-science, technology, politics, and culture-while lamenting the loss of kindness, nature, and purity. The figure views this shift in reverse, seeing how humanity advanced and simultaneously brought about its own demise, emphasising how actions affect the environment and life itself.

The recurring imagery of transformation-from destruction to creation, from chaos to harmony-underscores a deep philosophical reflection on the cyclical nature of existence. The cosmic figure ultimately appeals to a higher power, asking for wisdom to guide humanity and protect the Earth, which is portrayed as a precious, delicate gift in the vast cosmic sea.

The tone of the poem mixes a sense of cosmic grandeur with regret, reflection, and a yearning for redemption. At last, the cosmic figure, having completed their task, seeks rest, hoping that humanity will learn from the story and begin anew, crafting a future more aligned with the divine plan. The figure asks the Creator to start everything again, just like Adam and Eve, who, according to the creation myth of the Abrahamic religions, were the first man and woman on Earth and began everything. This means the figure himself ended everything and returned to start everything anew, becoming both the destroyer and the creator.

This work of art is a thought-provoking meditation on time, existence, and humanity's relationship with the planet. It balances themes of destruction and renewal with hope for the future, encouraging a harmonious rebirth for Earth.

|| अहं श्रेष्ठः, अहं अतिश्रेष्ठः ||

SUTRA 12

Burning Heart

It was a red dark bright day,
When a soul came to light, a hope of way.
A day of life, a day of warmth.
In my palm, a delicate soul,
A grain of rice, my finger's hold.

The day I rest you in my heart,
I thought you'd free me from the world's dark art.
A saviour, blessed from realms above,
A promise wrapped in endless love.
A beautiful life, God's finest art,
A saviour like the Lord, a gift from God.

The promise you made when you were small:
"I'll be the richest, proud and tall,
Make you gleam as dreams enthral.
No trouble will you ever see,
I am your shield, your park,
The bright breath dark, way out from forests heart.".
"No problems will you face,

I am your saviour, I am your soul."
When you spoke, a smile graced my face,
"Of course you will, why not soul."
Your words, a promise bright and clear,
Warmed my heart, chased away fear.
"You are my joy, my sweetest song,
The best of all, where I belong."
"You are my loving bird,
You are the sweetest of all,
You are the best, my dearest soul.".

"I am sorry my mom,
I failed it all,
I am worthless,
No use at all."
A voice echoed in this world wide,
Fading the sun, leaving its sight.
"I did nothing to make it real,
Lived in a world made unreal.
In my head, I did all bad,
Never tried to work hard,
Never tried to restart.
I did not turn our dreams into gold,
In a world too harsh and cold.
In my mind, I faltered there,
Never fought, never dared to care.

Father died hard, because of me,
To save me from the evil enemy.
I did nothing to save the great,
Just watched and let it all happen that day.
Why am I so bad?
Also, I too took the soul I loved the most,

The greatest of all, my creator, my Jan
anī.

The times I wasted, the dreams I shattered,
Not only mine but of us all.
The time has come to change it all,
The beginning of an end, the end of all.
Here I sit on the red roof tall,
Above this gleaming city like a god.
To make a wish last,
I am very happy to declare my laugh.

"I am the best, I am the bestest."
इति अन्त नूतनारम्भस्य||

DELVING DEEP

....

"Who is the greatest warrior in the world?"

"Have you ever thought?"

"Have you ever thought for whom you are doing everything, for whom you are living?"

This poem is not just a few rhythmic words, but it's a feeling-a feeling of every boy. It's about a bond, a bond greater than one with God; it's the bond between a mother and her son. It's a mirror of the harsh reality that: "Life can never be perfect."

This poem is about an unsung bond shared between a mother and her son. Whether we agree or not, being a female is a monumental thing, and women face countless struggles in this dark world. Their lives, though sacred, are often fraught with darkness, and that's the harsh truth of our heavenly earth.

At first, when the boy was born, he was like a flame of fire in a dark room for the mother-the only source of life in her wide world. She believed he would break her chains and lead her into the light of life.

As the poem flows, the perspective shifts to the boy's side. He has grown up, but remembers everything. He tries his best to change his circumstances but ultimately meets the face of grim. His father died because of him, and at last, he also lost his life-his mother.

In the closing lines, the boy is standing on the roof of the
tallest building in the golden city, and the poem ends with one
more end-the ultimate end.

96

|| संसारमृगतृष्णिका, हर्षः शोकस्य आवरणम् ||

SUTRA 13

Into the Dark White

Wake up, child,
It's time to die,
A whisper tickles in my heart's sigh,
To open wide my mind's eye,
A voice of life asking to die,
Making my breath sink,
And my lids comply.

The world is white in the dark heart,
See I saw nothing, nothing in sight,
In the void, no path appears,
Till the worlds start from the end, I stand,
No way to go, a world dark and bright,
The universe of life now a hellish white.

"Where am I, who am I?" echoes loud,
Emerging from winds of hope unbowed.
"Where should I go?" my heart did plea,
"To the last breath," she laughed at me.
"Is anyone alive?" my brain shouts loud,
And the world's floor breaks with deep dark down,
To swallow the hope and port us to life.

We're pushed back to reality, out of the brain,
From heart's world, mind's terrain,
A child stands, smile unfeigned,
New clothes, cone cap, joy contained,
In a room dark, happiness sustained,
Surrounded by smiles,
Ready to cut the cake of breath,
In the mind's eye.

DELViNG DEEP

"Into the Dark White" is a bewildering poem; it presents a profound paradox of outward joy masking internal realities, maybe framed within the context of a child's birthday celebration. The child is surrounded by smiles, but, unfortunately, unknowingly is inwardly alone. There's no clear path; everything seems right superficially, but inside, there's emptiness. It mirrors the experience of many humans who project happiness to the world while feeling alone inside their minds. The internal world is depicted as a fully white void, devoid of direction or purpose. This piece of art reflects the unsung dichotomy between external appearances of happiness and internal feelings of loneliness within most of us humans. At first glance, the poem paints a picture of a celebration—smiles, laughter, and cake. Yet, beneath this surface, it reveals a deeper, more unsettling reality: a profound sense of loneliness and emptiness that can accompany even the most festive occasions.

The child's birthday symbolises moments when we're expected to be happy and celebrate, surrounded by friends and family. However, internally, the child (and by extension, many people) feels isolated and directionless. Despite being in a room full of people, the child feels a profound sense of loneliness. This highlights the disconnection between external reality and internal experience of life. It shows that, from the top, it seems very beautiful, but beneath the surface, there can be a profound sense of isolation. The white void symbolises the lack of direction and purpose, a common experience for many who feel their outward lives do not align with their inner struggles.

This poem captures a universal human experience-projecting an image of happiness while grappling with internal voids and uncertainties.

The white void symbolises emptiness and a lack of direction, despite the outward brightness of the birthday celebration. This reflects the child's internal struggle with purpose and direction. The return to reality shows the stark contrast between the child's internal world and the external celebration. The imagery of cutting the "cake of breath" serves as a powerful metaphor symbolising life itself, which is celebrated externally but feels empty internally. It suggests that just as the child cuts the cake, the breaths of the child are also marking the slow, gradual passage of life. Eventually, the breaths will finish, and the soul will vanish into the sky and mix with the air, leading to an unsung end.

Ultimately, every soul will leave the body one day. It's a call to seek genuine happiness and fulfilment within ourselves, rather than relying on external validation. Otherwise, at one point in time, only souls will be left on the heavenly land-nothing else.

|| सुखार्णवे दुःखतरङ्गितं जगत् ||

SUTRA 14

An Beautiful Birthday

Happy Birthday, dear, with delight and cheer,
May blessings and joy fill your coming year.
"See they congratulate him, amidst the grand display,
In a garden of excess where shadows play."

"No, no, I don't want this."

In this vast abode, a miniature town, in the form of a house,
"Where my whole colony could settle down.
Also, leave a space for some to come,
A family or more to make it home.
Yet only three dwell in this sprawling grace,
0.01% of the whole in a lavish space."

In the endless garden, a celebration blooms bright,
Endless people standing in sight.
The party, a sea of red in the morning gloom light.
To celebrate only a birthday small,
Of a life one, but like a horde.
Candles blaze, balloons in red,

Carpets dyed in shades of dread.
Making it a sight to see,
From the eyes of my red bright glee.

Amidst the domes and colourless lights,
A boy's smile shines so bright.
"It's me do you remember hehe..."
Laughter dances, a festive tune,
Friends and family, under the moon.
Songs of cheer, a happy ruin.
In short, the boy's bright smile begins to wane,
Amidst the grandeur, a hint of pain.

The towering cake arrives, grand as can be.
The cake, like Everest, reaches the sky,
To cut it, they must climb so high.
To eat it all, they have to die twice,
A billion lives of breaths, a sorrowful treat.
But they are happy,
Their souls so bright,
Making their wishes to endless heights.
But shadows fall and smiles sway.
For a small reason like ants, but made big as clans.

Despite the grandeur and lavish sight,
The boy's joy turns to plight.
"This isn't what I wished for," he shouts,
Turning the festive cheer into doubts.

Parent's faces pale with shame,
Hearts burdened with guilt and blame.
The boy's cries, so harsh and loud,
Turn the cheer into a cloud.

Making a cry like he saw lots of food to eat,
Sitting on bodies of billion's breath,
In the rain red but food so tastes,
Let's eat it all then see the rest.

Outside the net, I stand unseen,
Witness to a scene so serene.
The night falls, the birthday fades,
And the birthday joy abruptly ends like shades.
Making an end with Everest falling down,
Killed few worlds lives in the form of ants.

But from the dark, a voice calls out,
"Hey, what are you seeing about?
It's late let's finish our work fast,
Or this time he will cut your head not your legs, haha."
"So collect it fast before you die.
I don't want to die so early by."
"It's your birthday, don't you see?
Collect fast or it will become your last breath."

But we can't celebrate like this, with glee.

"Come, the garden looks so grand,
Yet here we are, with dirty hands.
But we are happy because we are alive."
"Yes, only, on with garbage we stand, a leg cut off,
Wait, oh, my second eye has fallen let's find it off.
If I don't get it, how will I see, how will I collect garbage, only
with feel."
"Let's go quickly, sell our work and buy a treat,
A packet of biscuits, simple and sweet."

"This will be your greatest day,
So let's hurry, don't delay."
And I turn from the scene,
Leaving a mark of red dead hand on the garden's net bleed.
To find a joy that's small, but keen.

DELViNG DEEP

<hr>

"If someone is smiling, it does not mean the person is happy."

This work of art is actually a feeling, made from the heart and quoted with words. It is a poignant reflection on the dissonance between superficial celebration and genuine reality-the harsh, unsung dark reality. It is set against the backdrop of a grand but hollow birthday party. It delves into themes of materialism, disillusionment, and the stark contrast between public displays of opulence and personal dissatisfaction.

As the poem opens with a traditional birthday greeting, looking so beautiful, it juxtaposes a sense of irony. The grand celebration, depicted as a "garden of excess," contrasts sharply with the young boy's inner turmoil and dissatisfaction, who is also the narrator. The imagery of a "miniature town" within a house and the small percentage of people in a lavish space reflect the vast discrepancy between the grandeur of the party and the actual significance of the event.

The boy represents the true meaning of life. By seeing his appearance, it can be concluded that he is from a backward background-a place where death itself asks to die. He has to collect garbage to stay alive. He represents the children on the streets who face unsung tragedies during their childhood and experience great things at a young age. Those children don't know what the meaning of future; they don't know if they will get a chance to breathe again tomorrow or not. The boy's one leg was cut by a demon, also known as Homo sapiens, just because he may not have brought sufficient money that day.

He is also with his friend, who has also lost an eye and met the same fate. He is so hungry that if he gets food to eat, he will just eat it, forgetting that he is sitting on a mountain made not with stones but with billions of dead bodies-rotten, bloodied, and full of fungus. It's raining not water but blood, but the boy is so hungry that he cannot sense or see these things and just wants to eat, sitting on the soft bunch of beautiful fresh.

The contrast between the endless celebration and the boy's growing discomfort is highlighted through vivid imagery. The sea of red balloons, the towering cake, and the lavish decorations serve as symbols of excess and superficiality, but the boy is not happy. His joy turns to distress as the celebration feels more like a burdensome spectacle than a genuine expression of happiness.

As the poem progresses, the towering cake and the grandiosity of the event serve as metaphors for the inauthenticity of the celebration. The boy's lament about the grandeur of the party and his eventual realisation that the celebration does not align with his true wishes underscore the theme of disillusionment. His cries, which turn the festive cheer into a scene of gloom and regret, further illustrate the disconnect between external appearances and internal reality.

The poem shifts to a more surreal and grim tone as the narrator steps outside the scene, observing the stark reality of those working behind the scenes-the "garbage collectors" who, despite their grim circumstances, continue to work with a semblance of hope. The contrast between their reality and the grand celebration inside the garden serves as a critique of the superficial nature of humans.

The final lines try to bring a stark resolution. The disconnect between the grand celebration and the harsh reality outside is emphasised, leading to a reflection on the value of simple joys amidst overwhelming excess. The poem ends on a note of resigned acceptance, as the pure, holy, but dead soul acknowledges the contrast between the ostentatious party and the humble realities of life.

In essence, the poem uses the birthday party as a metaphor to critique materialism and superficiality, exploring the theme of genuine happiness versus the illusion of joy created by societal expectations. It serves as a reminder of the value of authenticity and the often-overlooked realities behind grand displays.

This poem is dark and sad, but it is the harsh reality of today's great world. It is a stick of truth on the face of human beings that: "Like whom you want to become is your dream, but how you currently live is someone's dream, so enjoy your life how you are, or you will live only in dreams."

The poem ends on a beautiful but thought-provoking note: whatever your situation, just enjoy life and live it just like the boy and his friend, is your struggle greater than theirs? At least we have the right to believe that tomorrow we will see the sun again. What else is needed? Everyone has problems; the rich kid also has his own struggles. So don't compare; just remember: "Sometimes, someone's life seems very easy, but we forget-this is life."

|| जीवितं यावत् तावत् जीवनं कुरु ||

SUTRA 15

Beautifull Breath

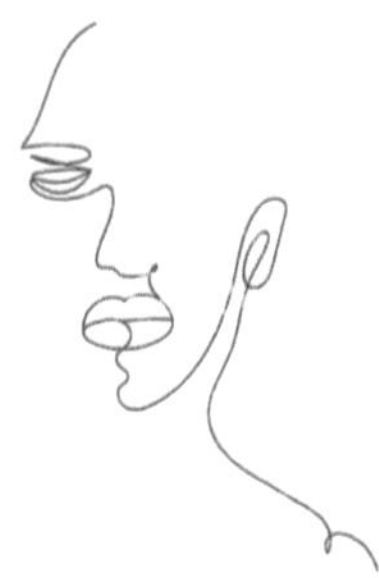

Oh my, it's ending at last,
Breath in stock, my escape so fast.
At last, a beautiful end,
Dreams carried away on the wind.
Amidst the chaos, where shadows collide,
He strikes the wall with a weary stride.

It's the tale of a man of steel,
Carrying countries on shoulders like wheels.
On the red field, resting to die,
To mix with soil. WHY?
Flesh full of blood,
Body full of pain.
End of one,
A beautiful tale.

Let's feel the pain,
Together in hell.
Of course, it's an interesting yell.

"Here, in this fractured world, I stand,
Breathing in the echoes of a life wide.
Time stretches thin as steel meets steel,
In these final moments, I deeply feel.
My childhood boy, such a beautiful flesh,
Moments of laughter till a cute rest.

The first ball on my face I grew,
My first crush, a cursed sue.
Rascals who shared the dawn's first light,
Their faces flicker in the edge of fight.

Parent's warmth, an affectionate embrace,
Oh, their soft voices lingering in sacred space.
Gentle hands, such a smooth touch,
Their memory etched tough, cherished so much.

Beauty formed in twilight's grace,
Love's tender gaze in a fleeting plate.
My joy, the sorrow, and every scar,
Bloomed me deeply, defined who WE are.

My mistakes, my trials mark my path of trod,
Each flaw, each triumph, every flawed facade.
In the ebb of life, both sharp and kind,
Yep, see the tapestry of what's left behind.

Did I leave something behind,
Or is it just my dream wild?

As the world dims, few breaths leave a soul,
One last exhale, and marks the end of a whole.

The battle's roar fades into the past,
A body left with a smile at last.

DELViNG DEEP

This poem is not just for a soldier but for every living entity. It's a poignant mirror of the end of life, capturing the essence of a person's final moments with a blend of nostalgia, introspection, and acceptance. It delves into themes of mortality, legacy, and the human experience, using vivid imagery and emotional depth to convey the inevitability of death and the memories that linger as life fades.

The poem begins with a sense of resignation and acceptance as the body approaches the end of life. The imagery of breath and escape signifies the finality of death, while the reference to "dreams carried away on the wind" suggests a release from worldly concerns. The mention of "shadows collide" and striking the wall with a weary stride evokes a sense of struggle and the culmination of a life spent in battle.

The central theme revolves around a person who has shouldered great responsibilities, symbolised by the "man of steel" who has carried the weight of nations. The "red field" and the question "WHY" hint at the sacrifices made and the pain endured. The poem reflects on the end of a life marked by both suffering and beauty.

As the poem flows, the individual reminisces about various stages of life, from childhood memories to the warmth of parents and the joy of love. These reflections highlight the contrasts between moments of happiness and sorrow, illustrating how they collectively shape one's existence and convert a group of flesh into a soul.

The exploration of personal flaws, trials, and triumphs underscores the complexity of the human experience. The final lines convey a sense of peace and acceptance as the end draws near, reminding us of the ultimate conclusion for every living being. The fading battle and the final smile represent a tranquil resolution, with the battle's roar and life's struggles becoming part of the past.

In essence, the poem offers a profound meditation on the end of life, celebrating the memories and experiences that define a person while acknowledging the inevitable passage of time. The imagery and language used evoke a deep sense of reflection and acceptance, making it a poignant and moving piece. The poem concludes with a universal line for all living beings: "Life is to live, so live it."

।। सन्ति प्राणिनोऽपि संवेदना ।।

SUTRA 16

Zoo Speaks High

Standing in front of hell,
I ask a question high.
Please, I seek the answer-
Don't say goodbye.
God, where are You? I am in Your home,
Want an answer, I am Your child,
Please give the answer, here I cry.
"Why did I die?"

It was a life so sweet, so calm, in the green embrace,
No worries, just laughter, and time to chase.
But then the world turned, a sudden plight,
The forest bled red, darkness swallowed light.
Flesh scattered, blood rained from the sky,
As Heaven itself seemed to burn and fry.

My mom was killed with bullets brass,
My father was filled with green grass.
I walked on hot stones and metals hard,
I cried but was left with nothing art.

Unarmed, I ask at the door of death,
If I was so bad, why was I born?
I lived for love, wanted for none,
Yet here I stand, my life's undone.

"Is this your tale, my dear, sweet child?"
"No, it's the world's-its cries run wild."

And with a gust of wind so cold,
We speed to the world's end, where stories are told.
Faster than light, we hear the calls,
Of every creature, great and small.

"I was taken and bound, my freedom erased,
For boots and trinkets, my skin tore off.
My skin was made into a mat so grand,
My spirit now silenced, a mark of your hand."

"People just think I look good hung.
Why do they forget that I also have life in me?
I was tethered, my life hung on display,
Yet my sorrow was real, in their cruel play.
Why must my suffering fuel their delight,
When my tears fell true, not just for their sight?"

Why must my suffering fuel their delight?
When my soul, too, has felt the night?
Am I a mistake, forgotten and small?
I, too, have life-I, too, feel it all.

"In the water, I flew, in shadows now lost,
Their progress, my suffering, at a grave cost.
They speak of their wisdom, of grandeur and might,

Yet forget the life they've snuffed from the night."

At last, a voice from beyond softly weeps,
"I wished to set right what the world so deeply keeps.
I crafted life with a vision so clear,
Yet find myself lost in the cries I hear.
I made humans, but perhaps forgot to sow,
The seeds of humanity in the hearts they show."

DELViNG DEEP

<hr>

"Have you ever thought about what would happen if animals could speak?"

"No? Let me tell you: if animals could speak, then the whole world would cry."

This poem delves into the profound mirror of the suffering of animals and nature, presenting a world where their silent anguish speaks volumes. It questions the inherent cruelty and indifference in human behaviour toward our living companions who cannot voice their pain. It paints a vivid picture of the anguish experienced by animals and nature, crying out to the divine for answers in the face of seemingly inexplicable suffering.

The poem opens with a child bear standing before the gates of hell, questioning the reason for its suffering and seeking an answer from the creator, asking a heart-wrenching question: "Why did I die?" The bear reflects on its once idyllic life in the forest, marked by joy and tranquillity, only to be shattered by sudden and brutal violence. The imagery of the forest turning red and the violent demise of the bear's parents underscore the devastating impact of human actions on the natural world. The bear's personal anguish is amplified by the broader context of a world filled with pain and loss. The tragic fate of the bear's parents and the child bear's suffering highlight the harsh realities inflicted upon animals by human hands.

As the narrative unfolds, the divine response to the bear's question reveals the divine inquiry, "Is this your tale, my dear, sweet child?" which is met with the response, "No, it's the world's." This shift reveals a broader perspective, amplifying the child's grief into a universal outcry. The poem accelerates to a cosmic scale, where the voices of numerous animals are heard, underscoring the collective suffering and plea for recognition of their pain. The acceleration to the world's end, where the voices of numerous animals are heard, emphasises the widespread nature of this pain and the urgent need for recognition.

The final lines of the poem introduce a sobering realisation: despite the creator's original vision of life and love, there may have been an oversight in instilling true humanity within the hearts of people. At last, the creator is also saddened and reflects that, with all the intent to bring forth life and love, they might have overlooked the importance of instilling true humanity within people and made humans, but may have forgotten to plant the seed of humanity in their hearts. With this in mind, the creator finally says:

"I wished to set right what the world so deeply keeps.
I crafted life with a vision so clear,
Yet find myself lost in the cries I hear.
I made humans, but perhaps forgot to sow
The seeds of humanity in the hearts they show."

॥ सुख-दुर्लभं हि सदा सुखम् ॥

SUTRA 17

An Unsung Beauty

In the pages of life, where stories are wrote,
This one is written with love, pure, holy soul.
Born from the depths of this world so vast,
Crafted by mind, yet shaped by my heart.
Not inked in books or carved in stone,
But breathed in love, where souls are known.

Once, in a place where dreams take flight,
Once upon a time, in a classroom's light,
I met a soul so gentle, so bright.
A calm breeze wrapped in human grace,
An angel from heaven, with a smiling face.

The world seemed new, colours more bright,
As if life had bloomed in a softer light.
The air felt fresh, the soil smelled sweet,
Yet-oh no, is that poop beneath my feet?
(Scratch that bit-life's still neat!)
For now, I see what God had in sight,
When He painted this world with warmth and delight.

Her eyes-deep as earth, rich and warm,
Cradling life in its tender form.
Her lips-roses kissed by the dawn,
A beauty where even angels fawn.
And there, that tiny mole near her graceful neck,
Turns the moon shy, makes it resign.

No, it's not just beauty you see,
But a soul so rare, pure, and free.
Born in this world once in four yugas, I say,
But this might be the first-and the last in any way.

Now, if you think this is a tale of love,
You're mistaken, dude-it's something above.
Oh, this isn't romance with butterflies,
It's a love that transcends, no room for lies.
This is the love that needs no fear,
For she's not just a girl-I hold her dear.

She's my sister, a guiding star clear,
Her name, a light that shines afar.
A word crafted by the hands of God,
Her name is "Sorry, there's no one."
"Is this everything in my mind, lol?
Of course not, this is to all my sisters, whole.
You're an art from the Lord."

So here's to you, my sister dear,
In every heartbeat, you're always near.
You're God's greatest work of art;
In the gallery of life, you shine apart,
A masterpiece that fills my heart.

"It's not all my heart does speak;
Yet, it's not my heart's greatest peak."

But all good stories don't have endings happy;
This one too met a fate of grim.
Lost a person more in this life so dim,
To become part of this faithless rim.
Misunderstanding misunderstood our misunderstanding;
At last, everything ended like a flow,
Like oxygen in winding snow.
न सर्वेषां सुकथानां अन्ताः सुखिनः न भवन्ति।

DELVING DEEP

This poem is a tale of love, an art created by the Lord Himself. True love transcends physical appearances and resides in the heart; it is this essence of love that this poem explores. It depicts a love shared by every human heart, one that does not require blood relations to be genuine and pure as heaven. This love can be expressed between anyone, not just family, embodying a universal and profound connection, an unspoken connection that can exist between any two pure souls. Yes, it's a love shared between a brother and a sister.

This piece of art is a gift to all my sisters. The central theme of the poem revolves around the tender and unconditional love between a brother and a sister, celebrated as a divine creation and a beautiful manifestation of pure affection. The art begins with a tribute to the profound impact of meeting a soul of exceptional grace and kindness-a moment that transforms the mundane into the extraordinary. Through vivid imagery and affectionate humour, the poem captures the purity and warmth of this bond.

The playful moment of stepping in poop, though seemingly trivial, serves as a charming juxtaposition to the deeper emotional currents of the bond, adding a layer of authenticity and relatability to the depiction of this cherished relationship. The poem beautifully blends warmth, humour, and deep emotion, reflecting the genuine and touching connection between siblings.

This poem blends light-heartedness with deep emotion, illustrating how even the simplest moments can hold significant meaning. However, the final stanza introduces a sombre note, reflecting on a misunderstanding and the inevitable challenges that can arise in any relationship. This shift in tone underscores the complexity of human connections, emphasising that not all stories, even the most cherished, end in unmitigated happiness.

It poignantly acknowledges that despite the love and effort invested, there can be moments of difficulty and loss, illustrating that: " Not all good stories have happy endings, but for happy endings, there should be good stories."

॥ अनुगचतु प्रवाह ॥

SUTRA 18

Grin of Paradise

Chirp, Trill, Warble, Tweet, Caw...
Sky's so white,
Stretching beauty to eternal light.
Sunkissed amber, glowing calm sight,
Warmth & love swimming till boundless psalm heights.

Cluck, Quack, Chuckle, Coo, Chirp...
With every chirp, a light takes flight,
The meadow dances in weaving bright.

Golden wheat sways, a rhythmic sight,
Stretching fields till eternal bright.
A highway of blue, a path unknown, till life to go,
Life flows freely, to lands yet sown.
Greenery all around, sky blue, a canvas anew,
Birds singing high in the unsung hue.

"Aaa...it's paining, bhaiya..."

"Please leave, I don't wanna play.
Leave me...aaaa..."
"Hmm...it's painful...haha...
Just once more, take deep."
"Na...aaaa...it's hurting," she weeps.
"I don't wanna play this game of blood.
It's disgusting, bhaiya, it's so dirty."

"It's not dirty, it's a game of art.
Take it hard, you will feel the weight.
Haha...it's so nice, isn't it?."

In a world where we live for love,
Lives a devil, a monstrous brute.
Attacks the one, eats the soul,
Makes the flesh burn alive.
Fills the pain, calls it art.

Flowing blood,
Through her nose,
Butt, neck, and toes.
"Haa...haa...haaa."
She tries to inhale,
As much pain as she can,
Blood of hurt, flowing through her veins.

In the heart of innocence, a blade strikes deep,
The laughter of a demon echoes where angels weep.
Among wheat fields' golden beauty, life begins to decay,
A soul's small voice begs, pleading, "Let me stay."

"Bhaiya, it hurts, let me go."
But her cries are muffled in the blood-soaked glow.

A river of red forms under her body's bed,
Flowing to eternal feet, weeping beneath a crimson shed.
Tiny hands claw at the mud below,
While a fiend paints horror where innocence used to grow.

Beside him, a tall girl watches, her smile a scar,
Eyes gleaming like shattered, corrupted pale stars.
Her laughter cuts through the child's scream loud,
Feeding the boy's twisted, monstrous dream shout.

The white sky turns crimson, clouds bleed ash,
Birdsong replaced by a vulture's laugh.
Screech, Scream, Hoot, Caw, Chirp, Coo...
The wheat stands witness, its stalks once green,
Now burning black in the unholy scene.
Turned dark ash, the black gold yean.

In the distance, a highway stretches to hell,
Where shadows dance, and no soul dwells.
The sky turns red,
The path turns black.
The scene of beauty a minute ago,
Becomes a scent of living hell to go.

The girl's voice, once soft, now cracks,
"Aaa...no...please leave me...oo...please."
An echo of terror that never comes back.

Her body lies broken, her soul torn apart,
An offering to darkness, a stain on the heart.
Once a petal of unsung future beauty,
Now turned to flesh of torn cruelty.
The mist gathers red, thick as sin,

A doorway to nowhere, where nightmares begin.

At the edge of the road, a figure sits still,
Clothed in white, yet feeling the chill.
Hearing the cries, his face tilts down,
Hands on his lap, his head covered with a frown.
"Aaa..."
As the cries fade into a soul of dim,
His robes turn black as the abyss within.
A silent witness to the world's attack.
Is it a game of tit-for-tat?

"I made this," he whispers, tears unseen,
"A place of love, now a devil's dream.
The beauty I created, with love in heart,
Turned to hell, as evil's art.
I created all to live in glee,
What's this mist inside of me?
The fields I nurtured now burn with hate,
The hands of life have sealed this fate."

His head falls low as the mist rolls near,
The weight of creation breaking the seer.
For the Lord is not absent but bound by despair,
A creator shackled by the monsters who dare.

The sitting soul stands, now ready to walk,
As the show of entertain has now turned stark.
The eternal reel of black stretches to the end,
Fog all around and mist-filled bends.
Walking on the road of happiness still,
A path made of bodies floating on all,
A road not of concrete or sand,

But of rotten flesh and red bodies spanned.

Lying stuck, thrown on each other whole,
Making a stack of a mountain red, tall.
The highway stretches, infinite and wide,
Carrying the screams of those who've died.
Path ending its run in the mouth of sharp,
The red black truth, Head of a rotten hungry Titanic maw.
Long teeth sharp wet, all smelly, black and dead,
Ready to chew more petals head.

And in the fields, where innocence fell,
A scar remains-a story to tell.
Bodies of all ages, if you dare to see,
All skin tones, all colours, spread brutally.

The eternal's clothes now turned black,
His whole body covered, face unseen back.
Walking on the road made of flesh,
One step on one body, the other on another's chest.
Walking to the red, in the white mist of pale feast.

अनुगचतु प्रवाह।

DELViNG DEEP

••

At first glance, "Grin of Paradise" would appear to everyone to be a contrast between the beauty of nature and the horrors lurking within humanity. However, beneath its poetic imagery, it reveals a chilling story of innocence lost, the cruelty of monsters hidden in plain sight, and a silent universe that watches but does not intervene. It attempts to paint a vivid and haunting contrast between beauty and brutality- The Dead Realities Of The Great Human Civilization.

It begins with idyllic imagery of a serene, golden landscape-a paradise of golden wheat fields, chirping birds, and the warmth of the sun stretching into a scenery of an eternal blue sky. This idyllic world symbolises purity, freedom, and the untouched beauty of life. However, as the poem progresses, this tranquillity is abruptly shattered. The golden warmth fades, replaced by darkness and bloodstained horrors lurking beneath the surface. RAPE. A sinister turn occurs as the poem delves into a disturbing scene of violence and abuse. A child is subjected to horrific torment, with her cries unheard and her innocence destroyed. The surrounding beauty becomes tainted with bloodshed, and the once serene landscape transforms into a nightmarish, hellish scene. With her every growing cry, innocence is destroyed, and the pretty, unsung souls take their steps toward the ultimate end.

At the heart of the poem lies the tragic story of a young girl, brutally taken advantage of by someone she once trusted-a brotherly figure. Her desperate cries, her pain, and her innocence being shattered contrast sharply with the backdrop of nature's serenity, emphasising the cruelty of the act. The presence of another figure-a girl who watches and smiles-adds another layer of horror, showing how evil can exist not just in action but also in silent approval.

As the girl's suffering reaches its peak, the landscape around her transforms. The golden wheat fields turn black, the sky bleeds red, and the bird's songs are replaced by the screeches of vultures. Nature itself bears witness to this atrocity but remains powerless to stop it.

In the final part of the poem, a mysterious figure sits beside the waving harvest, within which the tragedy unfolds-representing the divine entity or the creator himself. Dressed in white, he watches the tragedy unfold, burdened by the horrors of his own creation. He wants to stop this but has no other option than to weep for his creation and himself. His sorrow and despair reflect the helplessness of those who see evil but cannot undo it. As he walks away, his clothes turn black, signifying the overwhelming darkness that now consumes his world. An Art once created with love, care and happiness...not a mirror of Dead.

The poem ends with a haunting image: a road made not of concrete, but of rotten flesh and dead bodies, leading to an eternally unknown destination. The path ending its run in the mouth of the sharp head of a rotten hungry Titanic maw. Long, sharp, black-red teeth-ready to chew more petals and end all the endings of a beautiful future. This symbolises the unending cycle of suffering, the weight of sins carried by the world, and the eternal question-how does one escape from a world so tainted by horror?

At its core, Grin of Paradise is not just a poem about a single tragedy; it is a reflection of the hidden darkness within society. It forces us to confront the uncomfortable truth that paradise and hell often exist side by side, and sometimes, the most beautiful places can hide the most horrifying secrets. The poem's imagery and stark language try to convey the harrowing experience of the child, drawing attention to the horrific act of violence and the eventual death that follows. It's a tragic reflection on the brutal realities of the world, capturing the loss of innocence in the most unsettling way. The poem challenges everyone to confront uncomfortable truths and highlights the deep emotional and moral impact of such violence.

At last, the soft petal, who was once destined to become a beautiful flower and shape a great future for humanity with her intelligence and beauty, perished. And with her, died the great future of The Great Human Civilization. One who was going to make her tales of intelligence and beauty in the Golden pages of History with the ink of Gold...made it with the ink of red and became the memory of an unsung past. And with her died the Beautiful Future Of Humanity. Rest in peace...Happily.

"If we don't change, then nothing will change, and if nothing changes, then nothing will be changed. To shape the future, we must learn from the past-lest we fade into an unsung memory. If we turn a blind eye today, the time will come when this mother earth will cradle not humanity, but only the scent of its spilled blood in the soil."

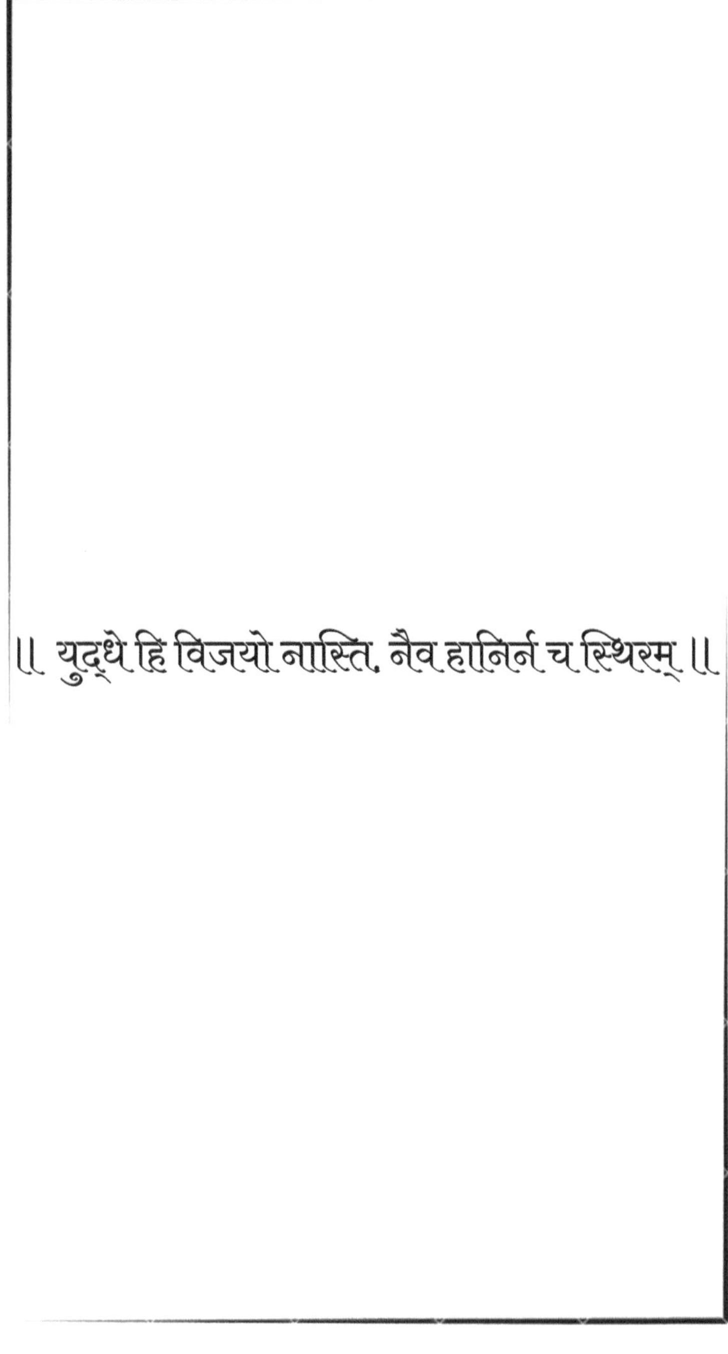

॥ युद्धे हि विजयो नास्ति, नैव हानिर्न च स्थिरम् ॥

SUTRA 19

Red Roses of HUMAN Art

"Is anyone alive..."
"Anybody alive...anyone..."
Walking on the bodies bunch,
Stepping on the red crunch.
The light of eve shining above,
The slept Sun, dazzling hub.
The huge of all, already dead,
The hue of red, around spread.

Eternal red lying around,
Lifeless roses died down.
One on top of another, No path to go,
A field of dead- the end of a show.

"Anybody there...hello...anyone..."
A call for them, who survived the art-
A Beautiful Human Art.

Stepping on flesh, to find the life,

After killing the souls, who once were alive.

A lifeless soul, holding a note in heart,
Living paper, peeping through the flap.
Glimpse of a beauty- A Real, Beautiful Art.

"When the war is over, and all,
We'll get married, our two half-souls will be one,
And the earth will grow flowers like you,
And your womb will carry the most beautiful girl in the
universe...in you."

(A letter found in the pocket of one of the ~~dead~~ soldiers,
1939.)

DELViNG DEEP

A battlefield turned to canvas, a war painted in blood-this is the art we never meant to create.

"Anybody alive...anyone..."- A voice echoes through the battlefield, fragile yet persistent, searching through the wreckage of war. But in a land where even echoes die, what answer remains?

"Is anyone alive..."-these are not just a few arranged words; they are echoes reverberating through the field of red- The Beautiful Battlefield, desperately searching for remnants of life amidst a landscape painted in death. "Red Roses of HUMAN Art" is not merely a war poem but a philosophical reflection on destruction, love, and the grotesque irony of human-crafted beauty-one sculpted not with paint and brushes, but with bodies and blood. We fight to live with our loved ones, yet we die, leaving them alone... For what? For a mere word-"LAND"..."My Land".

"Red Roses of HUMAN Art" is not just a war poem; it is a grim portrait of destruction sculpted by our beautiful human hands. It does not depict war as a moment in history but as a masterpiece of devastation, a grand artistic work where the only medium is suffering and the only colour is Red. The poem tries to immerse the readers into a landscape where beauty and horror have become indistinguishable, where the battlefield is no longer a place of strategy but of spectacle-a museum of lifeless bodies, each one a brushstroke in the final painting of humanity's self-inflicted doom.

At its core, the poem asks a haunting question: Are we artists or executioners? Do we create, or do we destroy? Are we mothers or murderers? Do we make life to bathe in their red pool?

*The Battlefield as a Gallery of the Fallen:

"Eternal red lying around,
Lifeless roses died down."

The poem transforms war into an art form, but not one to be admired. The battlefield becomes a garden of roses, not blooming from the soil but from the bodies of the fallen. The ground is painted in blood, each corpse a silent monument to a life cut short. There is no glory here-only a cruel beauty, an unsettling symmetry in the way death arranges itself.

Red-the colour of passion, of love, of life-is here the colour of death. Roses-the universal symbol of romance-are now symbols of ruin. What once stood for something beautiful is now a graveyard of unfulfilled dreams.

The war is over, but has anything truly ended? The dead do not speak, yet their silence tells a story louder than any victory parade.

*A Call to the Dead: The Echoing Void:

"Anybody alive...hello...anyone..."-These lines are the mirror of an unsettling loneliness. The speaker walks through the ruins, calling out, but the only response is silence.

- The repetition of "Anybody there" is like a heartbeat that refuses to stop, a last cry of desperation in a place where even echoes have faded.
- The phrase "A call for them, who survived the art" emphasises the twisted irony of war-only the dead have become part of this "art," while the living remains lost, wandering, searching.

*A Cry into the Void: Searching for Life Among the Dead

"Anybody there... hello... anyone..."

The voice calling out is not just looking for survivors. It is looking for proof that something once existed beyond war-for evidence that this field was once walked by the living souls, not just the dying. But there is no answer. The only response is the stillness of the dead, the cold embrace of a world that has lost everything and gained nothing.

Yet, amid the silence, one thing remains. Not a heartbeat. Not a soldier. But a letter.

*The Letter: A Love That Never Reached Its Tomorrow

"When the war is over, and all,
We'll get married, our two half-souls will be one..."

What can be the greatest tragedy of a story? A single piece of paper, tucked in the pocket of a fallen soldier-fragile, yet untouched by the carnage around it. It speaks of love, of a future that was supposed to exist. A promise made not to war, but to life.

This is not just a letter-it is the last whisper of a soul now lost. It holds the weight of dreams that were never given the chance to be fulfilled, of a love story that was never allowed to be written beyond its first page- Just One Page. The soldier who carried it into battle did not return, and the one who waited for him will wait forever.

The war did not just kill soldiers. It killed futures.

The date-1939-is a chilling reminder. A year when the world stood on the edge of annihilation. A year when countless love letters were never delivered, when countless promises became nothing more than ink on forgotten pages. A year when humanity decided, once again, that war was the ultimate art.

*The True Art of Humanity

"Stepping on flesh, to find the life,
After killing the souls, who once were alive."

The final lines deliver a brutal truth-we search for meaning in the ruins we create. We mourn what we destroy, we ask for life where we have ensured there is none. The battlefield is not just a place of death; it is a mirror, reflecting the worst of what humanity can be.

"Red Roses of HUMAN Art" does not simply depict war-it exposes it. It forces the reader(US-Humans) to stand amidst the wreckage and ask themselves:

- Is this what we call victory?
- Is this the art we wish to leave behind?

- And when we cry out, looking for life, will anyone be left to answer?

A battlefield is not a canvas. A corpse is not a sculpture.
Yet, again and again, humanity picks up its brush.

And the colour is always red.

*We stepped into the lord's light,
With blossoms clutched in hands so tight.
To honour the stone, to earn its grace,
Yet left a grave in nature's place.
Went to wash our sins away,
Yet carried another on our way.

|| अस्तीत्येवोपलब्धव्यः ||

SUTRA 20

Am I Alive?

Do you know, are you alive?

If you lust to swim among the stars,
In this boundless sky that knows no bars.
If your life is like a drifting kite,
Swimming in an unsung abyss of dark light,
Infinite wishes whirl within your heart,
But the path to truly live, you cannot find.
If aspirations lie buried deep within your brain,
Plight in the depths of your beating heartbeats.
If yes, if so,
Then, with hand upon your heart,
Ask a question hard,
"Am I Alive?"

If your existence seems like a colourless art,
Or an art with hues spread around.
If you exist, but no path in life,
Living like a puppet in a play live,
Lost in shadows, consumed by doubt and fear.
If you are ready to tear the dark light,
Yet the way remains hid from bright sight.

If you yearn to embrace life's infinite sea,
Yet the tempests of doubt pull you back, in mindless glee.
In a world where monsters lurk and prey,
Where anger and envy hold sway.
Where dark clouds obscure the great small sun,
Before so beautiful a sight to be seen,
Now it's flipping into a living hell.

Oh, sorry, I didn't intend to delve
Into the woes of the world in which we dwell.
My intention was to focus solely on you,
But truth slipped from my lips, a dark truth.
Fear not, let us proceed on this journey of life,
With determination and courage, meet skies.

If you possess all, yet crave for more,
If life's brevity leaves you starving encore.
If you dream of realms unexplored,
And seek a life in harmony with your accord,
Then, with hand upon your heart, implore,
"Am I truly Alive?" Let the question soar.

The answer, my friend, lies deep within,
No words need be spoken, no need to begin.
If so, cast off the shackles of rust,
Embrace life's lust, let your spirit combust.
Do as you please, heed not the world's decree,
For it is your life, yours to live, yours to decree.
If you merely exist, devoid of zeal,
Awaken now, let your essence reveal.
Break the chains of doubt that bind your mind,
Soar like a bird, let your spirit unwind.
Through the breath's expanse, let your dreams take flight,

In the embrace of the heavens, reach new heights.
Why linger in the shadows, timid and shy?
Embrace the vivacity of life, let your spirit fly high.

Why settle for a mere puppet's role
In the grand theatre of life, playing a mere stroll?
It's your life-live as life,
Why become a puppet alive in a play live?
Soar above the chaos, swim to the sky,
Listen to the echoes of your breaths, let them amplify.
Place your palm upon your heart, and there you'll find,
And will get a sound echoing in the blank rooms of your heart,
In the chambers of your heart, resounding endlessly.
Hear the sound you listen,
The reply will be:

"I am Alive."

DELViNG DEEP

<hr>

"Am I Alive?"

"Does this question ever arise in your mind?"

This poem is for every human being alive; it's a question for all who breathe: "If you breathe, does this mean you are alive?"

The poem is a profound exploration of existence and consciousness, urging every human to reflect on their life and ask the essential question: "Am I truly alive?" It grapples with the feeling of merely existing without purpose or direction and contrasts it with the yearning for a more meaningful and vibrant life.

The poem reflects the lives of most people, drifting aimlessly, much like an unsung kite in the winding wind, unanchored and uncertain. The imagery of "dark light" and the abyss suggests a world of confusion and unfulfilled desires, where aspirations remain dormant, waiting to be realised. As the poem progresses, the tone becomes more introspective, guiding us toward the difficult but necessary question that must be asked if one is to live fully.

Midway, the poem briefly shifts focus to the overwhelming challenges of the world-fear, doubt, and the darker aspects of human experience-before returning to a person's personal journey. This digression highlights the distractions that prevent one from embracing life's potential, reinforcing the necessity of breaking free from societal constraints and inner doubts.

The poem is a work of art that encourages every living being to seek self-empowerment and self-realisation. It calls for action, urging the reader to take control of their life, break free from the chains of fear and self-doubt, and live with passion and authenticity. The recurring motif of placing one's hand on the heart is a symbolic gesture of introspection-whenever there is a problem, simply place your hand on your heart and ask your best friend for the solution, and I am sure it will be correct.

The poem is a rallying cry for self-awareness, courage, and the pursuit of a fulfilled life. It tries to convey that one should listen to the inner voice that affirms, and strive to do something in life so that, one day, just once, they can place their hand on their heart and say with pride: "I am Alive."

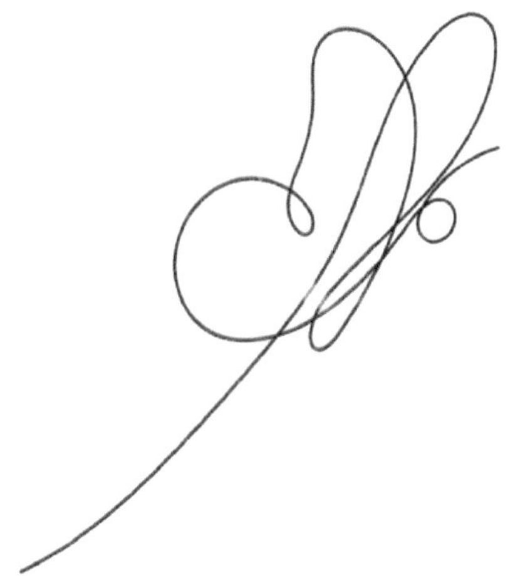

ACKNOWLEDGMENTS

I hoped to hold your attention for just a few poems, and I'm elated to say that I did.

Finally, I would like to express my heartfelt gratitude to a few special people in my life, without whom this book would never have come to life. First and foremost, I want to thank my real-life hero, my father, Mr. Ramashray Kumar Rana. From him, I have learned that life places stones in our path, but we must walk on them as if they were flowers. Over time, they will begin to feel like soft petals, and the pain will fade as we move forward. He has also taught me that life is a battlefield, and no matter how tough the fight gets, we must never give up-we must keep fighting until our last breath.

Secondly, I would like to express my deepest gratitude to my sweet mother, Mrs. Anjali Kiran, whose love has been my greatest source of reassurance in every difficult situation. Her unwavering support and strong words lifted me whenever I lost hope, and her encouragement played a vital role in the completion of this book. Without her motivation, these poems would never have become a reality. She taught me the true meaning of love, and everything I am today-whoever I am, whatever I am-is because of her, my guardian angel.

Thirdly, I would like to thank my cute little sister, Aaditi Raj, who never says she loves me but always shows it in her own way. Through her, I've learned that the truest form of love isn't spoken-it's felt in the little things, in the unspoken gestures that say more than words ever could.

Fourth, I would like to thank my friend, a pretty unsung soul: Disha. She gave me a piece of lifelong advice that continues to guide me in all situations: "Whatever happens, whenever it happens, don't worry-JUST CHILL." She taught me that no matter the problem, overthinking won't help-just chill, and you'll overcome every hurdle in life. Thanks for your quiet words, buddy. The first soul who saw that I am unique...someone special.
Keep smiling, Young Lioness-Always. Smile, Disha.

I thought of my these cute friends and sweet sisters while writing the poems related to sisters from a brother's perspective. Thanks, my sisters.

Fifth, I would like to thank my friends Prem Prakash Pashwan and Aditya Bhagat for sharing their valuable time with me free of charge and helping me complete this book by giving me honest and sincere feedback on my poems and correcting me when I made mistakes. From them, I learned the true meaning of friendship.

Finally, I would like to thank all my teachers who taught me how to read and write, shaping me into the person I am today. Their guidance made it possible for me to transform my imagination into a book.

(without their unsung help, these poems would never have been born into existence and would always remain in my thoughts. Thank you.)

ABOUT THE AUTHOR

Anand Raj Rana is an Indian author, artist, and multidisciplinary creator whose literary work spans novels, short fiction, and collaborative anthologies. Known for blending emotional intensity with poetic imagery and elements of mystery and imagination, his writing explores the quiet complexities of human relationships, inner conflict, love, loss, and the unseen layers of life that often go unspoken.

With multiple published books and a growing collection of short stories, Anand has steadily built a body of work that reflects both sensitivity and depth. His narratives often move between realism and lyrical storytelling, creating worlds that feel intimate yet expansive, personal yet universally resonant. Through his fiction, he seeks to capture fleeting moments, fragile emotions, and the powerful silence between words.

Beyond literature, Anand is an artist with a deep interest in music and technology. He spends much of his creative life sketching, learning musical instruments, singing, and coding-disciplines that influence the rhythm, structure, and imagination of his writing. This fusion of art and logic gives his storytelling a distinctive voice that bridges emotion with modern expression.

His debut work, *Die For Life: The Dawn Breath*, marked the beginning of his journey as a published author, followed by further books and contributions to multiple anthologies. With several upcoming projects in progress, Anand continues to expand his literary presence, experimenting with form, genre, and emotional storytelling.

Through every piece he writes, Anand Raj Rana aims to create stories that linger- not just on the page, but in the hearts of readers long after the final line.

Leave of a single second can leave you with a lifetime of regret. So, live every second, who knows next second you will live or not.